Leveling the Playing Field

Leveling
THE
Playing
Field

**WOMEN BREAKING BARRIERS IN
MAJOR LEAGUE BASEBALL
COACHING AND LEADERSHIP**

Al Lautenslager

NEW YORK

LONDON • NASHVILLE • MELBOURNE • VANCOUVER

Leveling THE Playing Field

WOMEN BREAKING BARRIERS IN MAJOR LEAGUE BASEBALL COACHING AND LEADERSHIP

Published in New York, New York, by Morgan James Publishing. Morgan James is a trademark of Morgan James, LLC. www.MorganJamesPublishing.com

Proudly distributed by Publishers Group West®

ISBN 9781636985459 paperback
ISBN 9781636985466 ebook
Library of Congress Control Number:
2024942649

Cover Design by:
Rachel Lopez
www.r2cdesign.com

Interior Design by:
Chris Treccani
www.3dogcreative.net

Morgan James is a proud partner of Habitat for Humanity Peninsula and Greater Williamsburg. Partners in building since 2006.

Get involved today! Visit: www.morgan-james-publishing.com/giving-back

This book is about inclusion, specifically the inclusion of women in Major League Baseball coaching and the front office. In view of that, this book is dedicated to the strong and courageous women in my life.

First is my wife, Julie Ann Lautenslager. I love the inclusion that she is part of with me. Next are my daughter Allison Lautenslager and stepdaughter Courtney Gessler. I also include my sisters, Karen Davenport and Pam Gatliff. Last but not least is sister-in-law Diane Prigmore, who is more a sister than an in-law.

All of these women have their own stories of strength, courage, living the dream, and inclusion, and that makes me very proud of this dedication. I love them all.

Table of Contents

Acknowledgments

This section is where I express my deepest gratitude and thanks to those who contributed to getting this book to the finish line and published. As I complete a book, I am always filled with a profound sense of gratitude, reflecting on everyone who helped me reach this point. It's time to spread some thanks. This part tugs at my emotions; my heart swells, and there aren't enough thanks to go around to my many supporters.

First and foremost, as always, is my wife Julie. She helps me reach any milestone in life. She cheers, motivates, and supports all my endeavors. Fortunately, we do it together, and that is gratitude at its finest. I love you, Julie Ann.

My daughter Allison is always by my side, whether physically present or from afar, emulating our shared philosophy of living the dream. This book is another dream, a labor of love, and a fulfillment of my desire to be creative, contribute, and share. Of course, in the background but equally important are Bradley and Courtney. I love you all.

Assembling a project like this takes a team, and they deserve a big "hats off." They make me look good as they elevate this craft to a new level. First, a huge thanks to David Hancock, the founder and publisher of Morgan James Publishing, the publisher of this book. David and I go way back, both studying marketing early on. My thanks extend to the entire Morgan James team.

Thank you also to Dave Swan, editor extraordinaire. He is truly an expert in his field and makes passionate writers like me look good.

A big thank-you goes out to the many women MLB coaches and front office leaders I interviewed: Kayla Baptista, Veronica Alvarez, Bianca Smith, Justine Siegal, Perry Lee Barber, Rachel Folden, Gretchen Aucoin, Amanda Kamekona, Katie Krall, Taylor Jackson, and Ronnie Gajownik. They were all instrumental through their insight, knowledge, and passion for the sport, their desire to help other women and to share their lives in the world of Major League Baseball with me. Thank you, and I look forward to your continued rise in the sport and watching you manage a game in person.

Little did I know that my early interest in baseball as an eight-year-old would lead me to this book. Pursuing different passions on a worldly basis has taken me to many parts of the game. I look forward to continuing this journey and sharing more with others.

All in all, thank you to everyone who supports me on my journeys. Thank you for allowing me to share and be gratified. I only hope that I can return the same to any and all in the future. Lastly, Nola and Ivy are always by my side in their own animalistic ways. They know I thank them—just count their daily treats.

And then there's Lu.

1. Introduction

In Major League Baseball (MLB), the realm of players, coaches, and managerial staff has long been dominated by men. However, there is a noticeable shift occurring, with an increasing number of female coaches making their mark at the professional level in the league, signaling a positive change in the traditionally male-dominated field.

In the rich history of Major League Baseball, a transformative journey is unfolding—one in which women are rising to prominent positions in the areas of team management, coaching, and leadership. Breaking through barriers, challenging stereotypes, and reshaping the landscape of the industry, these women are pioneers in a movement toward greater diversity and inclusion within the sport of baseball. This narrative seeks to capture the compelling stories, the triumphs, the paths, and the challenges of women ascending the ranks of MLB coaching, front office management, and leadership, exploring how their contributions are not only reshaping the front offices of teams and who is on the field, but also influencing the future of America's pastime.

These influences are all about thinking bigger and broader. It is also about action. Catie Griggs, President of Business Operations for the Seattle Mariners, said it best. "This is not an experience that is exclusive to the domain of people who grew up playing, who knew how to score-keep, who could throw and catch, or anything like that. Those people are incredibly important and core to what we're doing, but we need to be and think bigger and broader than that."

The transformation and the work yet to be done consist of providing resources, opening doors, and interviewing those qualified and interested, without the interference of gender. That thinking has led and will lead to overdue action.

In the early days of baseball, the managerial landscape was a domain dominated by men. The dugouts and front offices echoed with the voices of male leaders, while women were largely absent from these pivotal roles. This historical lack of representation for women in MLB management is exemplified by those who were told "no," refused the denial, and pursued their paths. Women being told "no" because of their gender is like a talented musician being rejected from a band because of their instrument choice. It's not about their skill or ability but rather a bias against something that shouldn't affect their participation.

As recently as ten years ago, when the baseball world was deeply entrenched in its traditional norms, passionate and knowledgeable woman named Kayla Baptista, Bianca Smith, Veronica Alvarez, Rachel Balkovec, Katie Krall, Kim Ng, Ronnie Gajownik, Rachel Folden, Gretchen Aucoin and so many more had a profound love for the game. Their dream, however, was not just to be a spectator from the stands. All of them aspired to be at the helm of a baseball team, involved in coaching or pursuing team management and leadership. Their in-depth knowledge of the sport, strategic thinking, leadership skills, and most of all passion were either fully present or in development. Yet the unwritten rules of the game seemed to have an unwavering stance against women breaking into managerial, leadership, and coaching roles.

A headline is usually considered a short, attention-grabbing summary of a longer story. Kim Ng's story shines through as an example of breaking barriers, leveling the playing field, and trailblazing a path for women in baseball coaching, leadership, and team management. Just look at the summaries, or in this case, the headlines published when Ng was announced as the first woman general manager in Major League Baseball by the Miami Marlins.

The Miami Marlins' hiring of Kim Ng as GM is a long-overdue breakthrough, and a great baseball decision

Kim Ng ready to bear the torch as baseball's 1st female GM

Story of Kim Ng is the (belated) story of baseball and America

Kim Ng makes MLB history

Kim Ng Has Been Ready for Years

Baseball told Kim Ng no (and no, and no) before it finally said yes

Headlines or otherwise, the women leading the charge of gender inclusion are tough and determined. They all reflect what Bethany Hamilton, an American professional surfer who survived a 2003 shark attack in which her left arm was bitten off and who ultimately returned to surfing, said: "Courage, sacrifice, determination, commitment, toughness, heart, talent, and guts. That's what little girls are made of; the heck with sugar and spice."

Ruth Bader Ginsburg also was profound in her belief, "Women belong in all places where decisions are being made. It shouldn't be that women are the exception."

Undeterred, these women tirelessly studied the intricacies of baseball strategy and statistics, sharpening their skills, making connections, and staying involved in any way, in the sport, with the hope that one day a team would recognize their potential and open a door. Despite their efforts, coaching and leadership positions remained closed to women like those mentioned and others. The prevailing belief at the time was that baseball coaching and leadership was a man's domain, and any deviation from this norm was met with skepticism.

Women have been playing baseball as long as men, with a rich history that includes pioneering figures such as Amanda Clement, Jackie Mitchell, Toni Stone, Maria Pepe, and Ila Borders. Although females were on the field, they weren't coaching.

It would take time and a shifting cultural landscape before women began to make inroads into MLB coaching. The story of these women serves as a poignant reminder of the challenges faced by women who aspired to break through the gender barriers in baseball, highlighting the historical lack of representation that has begun to change in recent years. It used to be that progress was slow and steady, but recently it has picked up momentum and speed. Again, there is still a ways to go.

Baseball can serve as a beacon to the nation, and increasingly, the world, beyond its pastime status. The game should be about equal opportunity, whatever the color of one's skin, whatever the gender or sexual orientation; an open door for people of differing national origin, with an understanding that everyone will play by the same set of rules and be accepted equally. It should be the custom and practice of everyday baseball life.

As our national game, baseball can and should define us as Americans, connecting us across all barriers. Add to this equal rights and opportunities and nondiscrimination. That's what we strive for here, today and every day.

A trip to the Louisville Slugger Museum and Factory, which I have visited, displays profiles and pictures of some of the women working in Major League Baseball.

Whenever you read about the announcements of Kim Ng as the Miami Marlins general manager in November 2020, the pictures showed her wearing a t-shirt with the words BREAKING BARRIERS emblazoned on it. Nike produced that shirt in honor of Jackie Robinson breaking the color barrier in MLB but in Ng's case, the shirt was very appropriate. Not only was she breaking barriers, but she was also on her way to leveling the playing field.

Those barriers have been broken, to the tune of having forty-three female coaches in the major leagues in 2023, the highest number ever recorded.

The title of this book is *Leveling the Playing Field*. The reason this title was chosen is because the definition fits the situation facing women in baseball coaching and leadership. A level playing field means a situation is fair, with no external forces affecting the ability of those involved to compete and be accepted fairly. In an ideal world, women entering MLB coaching, front office, and leadership would be judged solely on their abilities, not gender. Judging women because of their gender is an interference and would go against a level playing field with men participants in the league.

Merriam Webster says, "leveling the playing field," makes a situation fair for everyone, a total concept in fairness. It also suggests the chance of success is equal for all, male or female.

Leveling the Playing Field is a compelling book that delves into a transformative expedition and takes readers on an inspiring journey of women breaking through the traditionally male-dominated world of major league baseball coaching. The book provides a comprehensive exploration of the challenges, triumphs, and cultural shifts that have paved the way for women to take on pivotal roles within MLB organizations. This book serves as a powerful testament to the evolving role of women in a traditionally male-dominated arena.

II. Diversity

Importance of Diversity and Inclusion in Sports Leadership—The Call for Change

————

Diversity in baseball management, particularly at the MLB level, has been a common topic of discussion and has garnered attention in the news. The push for greater diversity and inclusion in MLB management is part of a broader societal and industry-wide conversation addressing representation and equal opportunities. Is the issue in baseball different than in other industries, businesses, or genres? The answer is it really isn't. Many argue that addressing diversity and inclusion in baseball is similar to addressing these issues in other industries or businesses. The key principles of diversity and inclusion, such as equal opportunities, representation, and creating an inclusive environment are applicable across various sectors, baseball included.

In the context of baseball, efforts are being made to promote inclusivity for women, both on and off the field. This includes initiatives to increase female representation in front office and leadership roles, support for women in baseball leagues, and fostering an environment that encourages participation regardless of gender.

It's important to note that progress may vary. Challenges specific to the sports industry and baseball, like traditional gender norms and historical barriers, can impact the pace of change. Overall, the push for diversity and inclusion in baseball aligns with broader societal efforts to create more equitable and inclusive spaces in various fields.

It's time to raise this discussion to a higher level of action, similar to the positive efforts and movement already taking place.

Was it because of Title IX?

The year 2022 marked the 50th anniversary of the passing of Title IX, part of the Education Amendments of 1972 passed by Congress and signed into law by President Richard Nixon.

The law reads, "No person in the United States shall, on the basis of sex, be excluded from participation in, be denied the benefits of, or be subjected to discrimination under any education program or activity receiving Federal financial assistance."

Joelle Milholm, staff reporter for *SB Nation*, a Colorado Rockies online community, reported that at the time of the amendment, many colleges and universities had quotas for women. The law was designed to end this discrimination. While it's mostly attributed to sports today, giving women more opportunity in the world of athletics was more of a fortunate side effect than the direct intent. It was a basic fact that sports at all levels—youth, high school, and college—were dominated by men. It's not that women didn't play or didn't want to; they just had fewer opportunities, especially as they got older.

Milholm went on to report that the passage of this bill, in many direct and indirect ways, was and is responsible for helping more women crack the world of baseball. Whether they were baseball players and lovers of the sport or softball converts, Title IX deserves credit for helping more women enter the MLB world, from fans and broadcasters to coaches, scouts, managers, and GMs. In 2022, the Colorado Rockies hired Emily Glass as the first female scout. Alyssa Nakken became the first woman to hold a coaching position on a big-league team when the Giants hired her in 2020, and the Yankees' Rachel Balkovec became the first female manager on an affiliated team this season when she took over the Low-A (minor league) Tampa Tarpons. All three women played softball in college. There are many just like them getting jobs throughout professional baseball who you will read about here. Was it due to Title IX? Maybe not entirely, but it sure helped and still is credited with opening doors.

Jenny Cavnar, who made history in 2018 as the first woman in twenty-five years to do play-by-play for an MLB national TV broadcast, said of Title IX around the time of the 50th anniversary, "I grew up playing sports and athletics—all the things that it teaches you and just how important having that in my life was. I am not saying that Title IX led me to the job here, but having those opportunities, getting to work in sports, being around sports, definitely opened the door. So, I am definitely grateful for that." By the way, Cavnar was named the primary play-by-play announcer for the Oakland A's, making her the first woman in Major League Baseball history to hold such a position.

A funny hint that Milholm went on to report references an NPR article. The article quotes former MLB infielder Greg Pryor as saying, "I came through baseball when it was very rare to see a woman in the front office or very visible as they've been in regard to baseball." Pryor, who played from the mid-1970s to 1986, remembers how women in the media were just then being let into clubhouses for press coverage. The only woman he said he dealt with on any team was Nancy Faust, the organist for the White Sox at Comiskey Park in Chicago.

III. Winds of Change

Shifting Paradigms—Evolving Attitudes Toward Women in Coaching and Sports Leadership

———

A lthough women have faced many challenges through-out history, they have come closer and closer to achieving gender equality in many areas, and those advances are not being ignored. In order for those advances to approach equality, there must be a shift in conventional thinking, a shift in paradigms. This means a significant change in fundamental concepts, experimental practices, and the way people think and accomplish tasks, overturning and replacing a previous paradigm. That is the case as it relates to women coaching, being in the front office, and holding leadership positions in Major League baseball.

In dictionaries, a paradigm shift is a situation in which the usual and accepted way of doing or thinking about something changes completely. That certainly is characteristic of the trend toward more women coaches and leaders in MLB.

Call it a paradigm shift, but an openness to diversity requires a shift in culture—away from good old-boys' locker rooms, sexual harassment, and definitions of the macho man tied to physical dominance. For those evaluating potential coaches in baseball, it means opening up their thinking and considering applicants who don't look or think like they do.

Fans and organizations alike will have to wrap their heads around a fact of gender parity in baseball coaching and start asking things like, "When we will see a female manager win a World Series championship?" That would be a leveling of the playing field.

To reach that moment will require many more women coming up through the ranks, ready to guide tomorrow's hitters and manage and develop future players. Increasing numbers of those women are already trying to mold the next generation. Keep reading.

Justine Siegal is a former MLB coach and the founder of Baseball for All, a non-profit organization that is leveling the playing field for girls across America by addressing the social justice issue of gender inequality. Siegal states, "I've never thought it was going to be a short-term effort. I think in five years, you'll see a major difference and you'll see almost all programs, all the major professional teams, having female coaches in some capacity."

When reading of new female coaches in MLB, reactions are often that these new hirings of women are the kinds of things that raise awareness, open people's eyes, and shift attitudes toward what is and should be happening. This is true, even though hirings are or at least should be based on the people, skills, and fitness, not gender. This represents a paradigm shift.

Leslie Heaphy, an associate history professor at Kent State University and the co-chair of the Women in Baseball Research Committee, attributes baseball's historical lack of gender representation to the game's origin. She said in a report to 19thnews.org, "The idea that women would be participating in something that represents so much of that manly tradition has been hard and made change difficult and that the emergence of softball in the 1890s and its modern perception as being an 'alternative for women' became another common argument used by opponents to keep women out of baseball. The only exception was during World War II and the following years when women played in the All-American Girls Professional Baseball League while many able-bodied men joined the armed forces." The culture that Heaphy speaks of was shifting, due to efforts within and outside of baseball.

The increasing number of women coaching in baseball is no longer an anomaly or exception. When the numbers grow like they are today, attitudes and culture change. That also represents a paradigm shift.

In the same 19thnews.org report Kim Ng, the first female baseball general manager, said, "It's about what has been accomplished for women. Confidence and desire and experience has been rewarded in the right way. It's about the path that has been paved and is going to continue being paved for other women behind me," which is another paradigm shift.

Alyssa Nakken, the first on-field female coach in baseball's major leagues, once told the Baseball Hall of Fame, "I think that there's going to be so many more women entering, not just coaching roles but also executive roles, in Major League Baseball and for specific teams. It's going to come fast, in my opinion. There are so many rock star women that are in baseball right now. It's just a matter of time that they start to get put into some elevated positions." If a paradigm is a standard, perspective, set of ideas or a particular way of looking at something, then what Nakken said is another indication of a paradigm shift in baseball.

In order to shift further, the importance of diversity of thought and diversity of perspective has to be considered. That sounds like common sense, but when diving deeper, different perspectives weigh out. That's what today's baseball teams are looking at. The progress in this is not linear and not often quick but it is happening.

When someone adopts a unique perspective, they gain fresh insights into something that others believe they already understand. This new viewpoint can unlock doors to enhanced performance and greater achievements in the realm of sports.

In order for shifts to be complete, there has to be less glamorization of the "firsts" and "the only" that are happening. Female leadership and coaching have to be commonplace. Talk, hiring and action have to be about the person or people involved, not the gender.

Veronica Alvarez, a coach for the Oakland Athletics, said, "I want to lose count of how many female coaches there are in the major leagues. If I do that, it means it is much more commonplace and that's our goal." That means that the paradigm has shifted.

Advocacy for Inclusion—Promoting Inclusion in Major League Baseball

The title of this section is Advocacy for Inclusion. Those words say a lot, albeit generally. More specifically, we are talking about promoting inclusion of females in Major League Baseball and in particular the coaching, front office, or general management component.

Advocacy is defined as any action that speaks in favor of, recommends, argues for a cause, supports, defends, or pleads on behalf of others. In this case advocacy for inclusion as we have spelled it out means actions that speak in favor of including females in the coaching, managerial, and leadership ranks of Major League Baseball. Boiling it down to the heart of the matter, advocacy is simply showing support. The bottom line is that advocacy is a powerful and important catalyst for change that is desired by all.

In conversations with current women professional baseball coaches, their advocacy for the inclusion of women in baseball is resoundingly clear. They live the results of this action every day.

There are a number of ways, not limited to these, to promote inclusion, support, and advocacy.

Advocacy Strategies:

- **Mentorship:** Encouraging mentorship is crucial. As more women assume coaching roles, they can mentor other coaches within or outside their organizations. This includes providing, where possible, internship or job shadowing opportunities.

- **Boost Confidence:** Many women hesitate to coach due to self-doubt. Building their confidence can help them overcome this mental hurdle. Seeing other women coaching helps others see that it can be and is being done.

- **Lead by Example:** Being living examples, with the goal of breaking barriers, can inspire others to do the same. These are increasing as we speak. It's just like any other leadership position: if others see what they want is being done, they can be fulfilled by this type of advocacy.

- **Share Success Stories:** Highlighting women's successes in coaching can motivate others to pursue coaching roles. These successes are growing every season.

- **Inspire Future Generations:** Women in coaching inspire the next generation to participate in male-dominated sports. This is usually part of their public message whether in the media or in person.

Advocacy can also include sharing inclusion-positive content on social media or by word of mouth, encompassing many of the items above. Showcasing specific individuals' successes, team successes, or progress in general is also advocacy. Veronica Alvarez, the coach for the Oakland Athletics who we will hear more about later and Amanda Kamekona, coach for the Cleveland Guardians, are just two proponents and examples of using social media as their approach to advocacy.

Networking plays a significant role in advocating for breaking the gender barrier and advancing to coaching, operations, or leadership positions. Currently many female coaches talk amongst themselves or in group functions, usually advocating and promoting inclusion.

Acceptance of women in male-dominated sports often depends on leadership. Those women who are coaching now and have been accepted into the league are identified by other females as leaders. Leadership provides a platform for advocacy.

Justine Siegal, mentioned earlier, advocates for gender equity in sports through her organization, which focuses on developing positive youth coaching practices and increasing access for young girls.

Organizations like WeCOACH actively recruit more women coaches through workshops and programs to build a pipeline of future leaders. WeCOACH is dedicated to recruiting, advancing, and retaining women coaches in all sports and levels through professional growth and leadership development programs.

MLB has made significant progress in diversity and inclusion through efforts like Employee Resource Groups (ERGs). The groups, which were launched in 2017 by the MLB central office, are voluntary and employee-led. Their aim is to foster a sense of camaraderie, community, and learning, alongside a diverse and inclusive workplace that aligns with the values of the sport. Many teams now have them.

One standout group is the MLB Women ERG, which aims to cultivate an inclusive environment that inspires women to advance their leadership potential through networking and mentorship.

Many teams also have events and programs devoted to diversity and inclusion. For example, the New York Mets host Women's Day at Citi Field. This event, led by the Mets' female-driven employee resource group "She-Unit," celebrates women in sports with pregame and in-game programming in honor of Women's Equality Day.

The Mets created Employee Resource Groups to strengthen bonds among employees who share common causes or interests. Participation in ERGs cultivates a workplace where everyone feels a sense of belonging, promotes cultural awareness, and fosters innovation. The Mets are dedicated to building a diverse and inclusive culture, both on and off the field, where ERGs positively influence employees, fans, and communities.

Many MLB teams have people in advocacy positions in place. For example, the Atlanta Braves have an executive vice president and chief culture officer. At the time of this writing, the person in this position was DeRetta Rhodes, who is proud to say that she has a passion for people, leadership and dreams realized.

While this book is about women in major league coaching, there are advocacy efforts going on at the minor league level as well. As stated on their website (milb.com):

> *"Minor League Baseball has placed diversity and inclusion at the forefront of its growth strategy. We strive to create an industry where all identities are represented, welcomed, valued, and empowered to enhance our league's culture, creativity, innovation, and comprehensive service to the communities we occupy. We strive to be the most fun and inclusive league in all of sports and entertainment. While conversations regarding diversity and inclusion happen daily in the Minor League Baseball office and among our 160 clubs, we recognize the need to do more to elevate the voices and stories of those who currently work in our industry.*
>
> *The goal is to spotlight the people, programs, and stories in MiLB that champion diversity and inclusion and advance the mission of Minor League Baseball's diversity initiative."*

Though the league (MiLB) focuses on and dedicates time and effort to its diversity and inclusion goals, there is, as it states, "…work to be done on the front of equal gender representation in the industry. The number of women employed by MiLB teams is growing, and Minor League Baseball recognizes the opportunity to embower those women in the way of career advancement."

Billie Jean King, a tennis legend and minority owner of the Los Angeles Dodgers, has significant aspirations for enhancing women's involvement in baseball. King, a thirty-nine-time grand slam champion, joined the Dodgers ownership group alongside her partner, doubles champion Ilana Kloss, with ambitious plans for the historic ball club. Her passion for baseball and softball adds depth to her commitment to fostering inclusivity within the Dodgers community.

King expressed her hopes for the future by stating, "Hopefully, to encourage girls to be in baseball and softball, we've got to figure that out." She emphasized the importance of total inclusion, saying, "But we want everyone to be a part of the Los Angeles Dodgers; we really think it's really important to have total inclusion." This includes women players, but it starts at the coaching level. There are female coaches now. There are no female players yet.

MLB's Diversity Pipeline Program creates learning and experience for applicants through various initiatives, including the Society for American Baseball Research (SABR) Analytics Conference, the Diversity Pipeline Scout and Coaching Development Program, the Take the Field program, and MLB Partner Leagues (for example, the Appalachian & Draft League) throughout each summer.

Incorporating diverse perspectives is crucial for progress. The leaders of Major League Baseball have stated that the organization recognizes this and is committed to diversity, equity, and inclusion in the workplace and beyond.

In an article by Stanley Kay in *Sports Illustrated* on August 19, 2016, Justine Siegal, a member of SABR and the first woman MLB coach, shared her childhood affinity for *Peanuts* comics. Despite the iconic status of characters like Charlie Brown and Snoopy, Siegal found a special connection with Peppermint Patty.

Peppermint Patty, introduced by Charles Schulz in 1966, quickly became renowned as the best athlete in the strip, regardless of gender. She managed a baseball team just a few years after girls in America gained the right to play Little League.

Siegal, who made her MLB coaching debut with the A's in 2015, didn't initially realize the trailblazing nature of Peppermint Patty. Schulz's portrayal of her made gender equality in sports seem normal.

As suggested by the title of the *Sports Illustrated* article, "How Peanuts' Peppermint Patty became a fierce advocate for female athletes," Peppermint Patty is an unexpected champion of women's sports, a fictional but powerful advocate for women and girls in a sports world dominated by men.

Schulz's portrayal of Peppermint Patty as a strong female athlete had a profound impact. Jaime Schultz, a

Penn State professor of kinesiology who studies the history of women in sport, noted that Schulz not only reflected the times but provided a role model that challenged traditional stereotypes, potentially changing the way people viewed athleticism.

Peppermint Patty's influence continues to resonate. So does Justine Siegal's. Their character serves as a reminder of the importance of representation and advocacy for women in sports, inspiring generations to challenge gender inequality on the field. A win for women in sports.

IV. Navigating Challenges

Breaking Stereotypes: Addressing Gender Biases in the Baseball Industry

ender parity is a longstanding issue. Historical records consistently highlight instances of women facing inequalities in various aspects of life, including their careers, education, and homes. Sports, including the coaching profession in baseball, are no exception. The perceptions of dominance, physical strength, and power typically associated with men have often resulted in exploitation, exclusion, and discrimination for women. Overcoming these stereotypes remains a significant challenge.

There are several ways to address and encourage gender equity in the sporting world, including bringing female coaches into baseball. Before putting solutions into practice, a few gender bias ground rules need to be established by any team, organization, or leadership group. Consider the following:

- People automatically think men are the only ones who can be in coaching and leadership. That thinking shouldn't be automatic. Stop assuming men are superior athletes and coaches and that only men belong in coaching, leadership, and management.

- The number of women in baseball is rising. That may be unknown to many people but it is a fact. Find one or more women to represent and promote female role models. Find a way to celebrate female participation in the sport.

- Learn to recognize where and when gender bias is happening. This could almost be called a gender bias audit, and is something every team and organization needs.

- Practice self-inspection: Check your own interactions, conversations, and actions for bias.

- Understand and use your platform to communicate and influence.

- Share learning. Speak up and spread the word of positive actions that overcome gender bias.

Another action that easily can be added to the list is not letting sports marketing overrun opinions. Audit media choices for their fair practices and boost media exposure where appropriate and applicable.

Media representations of sports and athletes often reinforce harmful gender stereotypes by portraying women athletes primarily as women rather than as athletes. The media's influence is profound, shaping societal attitudes, beliefs, and practices, often without awareness. Collaborating organizations and the media can leverage their power and voice to increase visibility for women in sports and address inequalities in sports and journalism, a practice often referred to as using a platform.

Gender parity has been a longstanding issue, evident in historical records documenting women's struggles with inequalities in various aspects of life, including their careers, education, and homes. Sports, unfortunately, are no exception. The traditional portrayal of men as dominant, physically strong, and powerful has led to violence against women, exploitation, exclusion, and discrimination. This narrative must change.

Sports have historically been associated with men and their interests, further perpetuating gender disparities and alienating women. There are several ways to encourage gender equity in the sporting world, including:

- **Support the gender as a fan or player.** For the general public and those who want to be involved in sports and baseball in the future, support women's and girls' sports as a fan or player. Support can come in the form of attending women's sports events at all levels. This applies to everyone, male, female, young and old. Continue to play a sport that interests you and play baseball if that is your athletic dream. Support female athletes by watching their games or following them on social media. Learn, understand, and cheer along the way.

- **Develop gender equity policies.** All sports organizations need to work toward gender equity. Women in sports should have equal participation opportunities, funding, wages, benefits, and jobs. Putting these goals into policy is progress toward gender equity.

- **Be cautious of language used in communications.** Avoid sexism. When writing or speaking about women's sports, don't use innuendos or belittle athletes by alluding to their appearance or family roles outside the game. Use similar vivid language when describing both female and male athletes' actions and performances.

- **Allow for a mechanism for opinions and suggestions.** Some call this whistleblowing, which is usually negative. However, opinions and suggestions can be positive and healthy. A mechanism like this can also be used to share ideas, voice concerns, and offer opinions.

- **Hire more females in sport, coaching and front offices.** Encouraging women to pursue careers as players, coaches, trainers, front office staff, and sports journalists can push sports and baseball toward gender equity. Whether given informally or through organized programs or efforts, encouragement should be very visible. Hiring can come from this.

- **Don't assume men are superior athletes.** Another way to promote gender equity in sports is to stop portraying men as stronger, better, and faster than other genders. Women have unique strengths and skills and may be superior to men in some instances.

- **Disregard talk of masculinity.** Don't just glamorize the male gender in sports. Baseball should not be a way for boys and men to prove their masculinity. In the world of females in baseball, this shouldn't even enter the conversation. To make it plain and simple: the exclusion of girls and women from the national pastime because of gender, whether playing, coaching, or managing, **should not exist.**

Reiterating a crucial point: To advance equity in sports, equal opportunities must be available to athletes of all genders. Achieving gender equality in sports requires the active involvement of everyone. Individuals should be mindful of words and actions that may unintentionally perpetuate gender inequality. When discussing gender equality on social media, it's important to use inclusive language and exercise caution. Seek out materials and information on how others are promoting gender equity in sports.

As Nelson Mandela famously said, "Sport has the power to change the world. It has the power to inspire. It has the power to unite people in a way that little else does.

It speaks to youth in a language they understand. Sport can create hope where once there was only despair."

Coaching is a pivotal opportunity to shape the perception of the sport and its athletes. A good coach can elevate an athlete's performance, and the more diverse the coaching staff, the better the environment for athletes. This applies equally to female athletes and a baseball team's coaching staff.

Stories of resilience and determination—Overcoming obstacles

This book and the title emphasis would not be complete without a mention of women breaking into a league of their own in the 1940s. Yes, it is about playing baseball, but the spirit is alive in coaching and managing teams. By now, most of those interested in the sport of baseball have heard of the blockbuster movie *A League of Their Own*. To this day, *A League of Their Own* continues to charm and intrigue audiences with its inspiring storyline. The story takes viewers on a journey through the trials, tribulations, victories, and celebrations of the All-American Girls Professional Baseball League (AAGPBL).

More than just a sports movie, *A League of Their Own* explores the whole concept of breaking down barriers. The film celebrates the resilience, determination and passion of the women who played in the league and their impact on baseball.

During a time when gender stereotypes loomed large, the women encountered significant challenges. Players confronted prejudice, skepticism, and discrimination, often facing criticism that playing baseball would undermine their femininity. Yet these remarkable women defied societal expectations and demonstrated their excellence in the sport they cherished. Breaking gender barriers defies social expectations of all sorts.

The All-American Girls Professional Baseball League played a crucial role in paving the way for women in sports and baseball in particular. It showcased women's ability to compete at a professional level, defying the notion that sports and baseball were only for men. Its impact continues to be felt today, inspiring generations of female athletes to pursue their baseball aspirations.

The women of the league were not only outstanding athletes but also dedicated, committed, resilient individuals. They endured grueling schedules, lengthy road trips, challenging playing conditions, gender backlash, and more. Despite these obstacles, they exhibited their skills and love for the game, pursuing a passion and leaving behind a lasting legacy. Gender had nothing to do with them excelling in the sport and in the league.

The league's pioneering efforts established the groundwork for future generations of female athletes, demonstrating that women could thrive in sports that had traditionally been male dominated.

One of the league's esteemed teams, the Racine (Wisconsin) Belles, stood out as a symbol of determination and resilience. Life as a Belle went beyond the baseball field, shaping the lives of these remarkable women with opportunities to travel, earn money, and play a male-dominated sport. The Racine Belles' legacy extended far beyond base-ball, showcasing the power of determination, camaraderie, and breaking societal barriers to pursue their passion. Their accomplishments and struggles paved the way for women in sports, leaving a lasting inspiration for today's athletes. The example of female athletic prowess set forth by the AAGPBL-inspired movements, at the time, to advance women's athletics worldwide. According to the newsletter *Dirt In Their Skirts: The All-American Girls Professional Baseball League*, the league, "provided an important precedent for later efforts to promote women's sports," most famously the creation of Title IX in 1972.

Again, the legislation stated that, "No person in the United States shall, on the basis of sex, be excluded from participation in, be denied the benefits of, or be subjected to discrimination under any education program or activity receiving Federal financial assistance." The passage of Title IX, combined with a new passion to provide women with equal athletic opportunity, created a shift in the way gender roles are accepted and a change that molded today's society. A big thank-you is owed to the All-American Girls Professional Baseball League in this regard.

We hear today from coaches that even though there are obvious gender issues at times, they truly don't think about it and go on about their business regardless of gender. Toni Palermo, a former women's league player, said, "I did not think I was pioneering because I always [played baseball], but as I look back now, it absolutely opened doors."

While still not a women-in-coaching story, women playing the sport offer the perspective of overcoming obstacles and how gender challenges were faced. Toni Stone's story is one of overcoming immense obstacles in the world of baseball. While the All-American Girls Professional Baseball League is often celebrated for its role in women's baseball, it was unofficially segregated, excluding non-white players. There's a brief scene in the movie that highlights a remarkable throw by a Black woman, hinting at the unfairness of this exclusion.

Despite the league's success, female players of color remained largely unseen, as they faced the dual challenge of racial and gender discrimination. Toni Stone shattered both barriers by playing in the Negro Leagues, challenging the notion of women as, "the weaker sex."

Stone made history in 1953 by becoming the first woman to play regularly on an American major-level professional baseball team, the Indianapolis Clowns, in the all-male Negro Leagues. She later played for the San Francisco Sea Lions, the New Orleans Creoles, and the Kansas City Monarchs.

Stone encountered taunts and resistance from teammates and opponents alike. Despite this, she persevered, even reportedly hitting a single off a fastball thrown by the legendary Satchel Paige during an exhibition game. Her presence drew record attendance to Clowns games and was prominently featured in the team's promotional materials.

Despite her popularity with the fans, Stone faced hostility and exclusion from male players and management, enduring challenges like being denied access to locker rooms and pressure to play for sex appeal. Bunny Downs, the manager of the Clowns, had reportedly once told Stone that, "she'd better stick to knitting and home cooking," but publicly claimed to be won over after seeing her play. Most of the male ballplayers shunned her and gave her a hard time because she was a woman. Stone was quite proud that she was a target and they were out to get her. She would show off the scars on her left wrist and remember the time she was spiked by a runner trying to take out the woman standing on second base. "He was out," she recalled.

Even though she felt like, "one of the guys," the people around her did not accept her as one. While playing for the Kansas City Monarchs, her time on the bench was spent sitting right next to the men who hated her. "It was hell," she said.

Despite the hardships, Stone remained steadfast. Her contract was eventually sold to the Monarchs, and she retired after the 1954 season due to lack of playing time. Her legacy as a pioneer in women's and Black baseball lives on, inspiring future generations to challenge barriers and pursue their dreams. (Source: Wikipedia).

This is just a sampling of the many related examples. As more females enter into the sport and their presence becomes more commonplace, their stories will be about sports and baseball, not gender.

Although the AAGPBL and the Toni Stone stories are more about female players than coaches, the emergence of female trailblazers in baseball reflects the evolving dynamics of the sport. From Toni Stone to contemporary inspirations like Mo'ne Davis (a former Little League pitcher), women are demonstrating their rightful place on the field. The ongoing expansion of women's baseball leagues and the achievements of female players across different levels highlight the significance of dismantling gender barriers and fostering inclusivity in one of the world's most beloved sports. As we recognize these innovators, we look forward to a future where gender no longer limits a player's role on the field, whether playing or coaching, making baseball a sport accessible to everyone.

Lessons Learned: Insights gained from navigating the challenges of women in the MLB

A common-sense steppingstone for women athletes is to have women coaches in baseball. Fortunately, the number of female coaches in Major League Baseball is on the rise.

Sport holds immense visibility and is among the most influential social institutions. Individuals in sports, especially coaches, communicate a powerful message about what is deemed relevant and valued, as well as what is not. They have a powerful platform. The statistics and real life reveal that coaching positions are predominantly held by men. There are lessons to be learned from both positive and negative examples and there is potential to boost the number of female coaches in the field.

One lesson is that as the number of women coaches grows, they will bring other women into the profession.

Nicole Lavoi reported, based on research for her book *Women in Sports Coaching*, these other lessons of females in coaching:

- When men witness women excelling as athletes or players in sports, they tend to develop greater respect for them in other aspects of life, such as work, friendships, and intimate relationships.

- Women coaches advocate for other women, while when women are "out of sight" they're "out of mind" and their needs don't get prioritized. This situation changes when there are enough women decision-makers.

- Female coaches are significant to other women in coaching as they offer support and guidance on navigating a traditionally male-dominated workplace.

- Lavoi writes, "By increasing the number of women coaches, we can change perceptions, give equitable opportunities, and positively influence the lives of young women. We are poised to change the landscape not just for current coaches, but also for the next generation of aspiring female coaches."

- How the "people side" of sport is handled directly impacts whether a team wins or loses.

- A successful coach is positive, enthusiastic, supportive, trusting, focused, goal-oriented, knowledgeable, observant, respectful, patient, and a clear communicator. These qualities result in productive players, better player-coach relationships, and attainment of overall goals.

In a recent interview at the major league spring training camp, young minor league players indicated their female coaches were very knowledgeable, well-liked, and their approach and knowledge appeared to be better than what some of the male coaches possessed. This is a profound result of lessons learned along the way.

Sports Marketing Progress Toward Gender Parity

In recent years, the sports industry has made significant progress toward achieving gender parity in its marketing efforts. One notable advancement is the increased visibility of female athletes, who historically received less coverage than men. Today, female athletes are gaining more attention, endorsement prospects, and representation in marketing campaigns, challenging the perception that sports are predominantly for men.

Sports marketing has undergone a profound transformation, expanding beyond conventional boundaries to adopt a more equitable and inclusive approach. This includes a commitment to gender parity, reflecting the global push for greater gender equality. The recognition of the significance of equal representation and opportunities in sports marketing is not only a moral imperative but also a strategic decision that brings several benefits.

Firstly, it aligns with the values of inclusivity and diversity, appealing to a broader audience and fostering a positive brand image. Consumers are increasingly conscious of social issues and are more likely to support brands that align with their values. Moreover, gender equality in sports marketing can help cultivate women as influential leaders in sports, an area where they have been historically under-represented.

The rise of women in sports, both as athletes and spectators, has been accompanied by a growing recognition of women as consumers. Brands have responded by featuring sportswomen in their advertising campaigns, recognizing the value of targeting women in their marketing strategies.

Gender parity in sports marketing is not just a passing trend but a reflection of the evolving landscape. As brands continue to prioritize inclusive and equitable campaigns, the path to gender equality in sports marketing becomes clearer. By breaking stereotypes, promoting diversity, and investing equally in athletes of all genders, the sports industry can inspire positive change, encourage broader engagement, and create a more inclusive future.

V. Pioneering Figures
Trailblazers Entering MLB

———

The number of women in baseball coaching, front office, and management positions is at an all-time high and is growing. Credit goes to those who laid the groundwork for their own as well as future generations. Learning about their paths, their challenges, their talents and skills and their advice will help other females interested in following a similar direction. This chapter highlights these early and formidable trailblazers.

Kayla Baptista—A Quick Path and a Championship Ring

When diving into the subject of women in sports and their paths—past, present, and future—why not talk to someone who has the big goal? That goal is to become a major league baseball team manager. There are no bones about Kayla Baptista's goal.

Kayla Baptista's ambition of becoming a manager is a powerful statement in a field where women have historically been underrepresented. Her determination to break through barriers and reach the pinnacle of her profession is not only a personal aspiration but also a significant stride toward gender inclusivity in the world of Major League Baseball.

By openly declaring her goal, Kayla is not only setting a high standard for herself but is challenging the norms within the baseball community. The role of a manager in Major League Baseball is highly prestigious and comes with immense responsibilities, as it historically is a position held by men. Kayla's ambition reflects a broader movement for gender equality and representation in sports leadership roles.

Her willingness to share this goal with anyone who will listen speaks to her confidence, passion, and commitment to creating a path for future generations. As she pursues her dream, Kayla not only aims to manage a team but also hopes to inspire and pave the way for more women to follow. Her journey serves as a beacon of hope for those aspiring to break gender barriers in the sports industry and emphasizes the importance of setting ambitious goals to drive meaningful change.

Meet the 22-year-old Rhode Island woman living her pro baseball dream.

Kayla Baptista became a baseball fan at an early age. She grew up in Rhode Island in a family of season ticket holders for the nearby Boston Red Sox. Their AAA affiliate played in Pawtucket right next to her dad's office. Kayla and her family attended several games a month there. To say she was and is a huge Red Sox fan would be an understatement. That all shows in pictures of her at a very young age at Fenway Park, where Kayla watched her heroes vying for and winning a world championship. She recalls seeing players hoisting the World Series Championship trophy, getting giddy like all true fans do. She remembers shouting, "I want to do that too someday."

Kayla didn't start out playing baseball, as girls' softball was an easier avenue at the time, and is a familiar path for many females breaking into baseball. That propelled her to play at the Division 1 level at the University of North Carolina. Her playing career was cut short by injury but evolved into joining the coaching staff at UNC. Before that, though, she had a coaching stint with 297 Baseball Academy in Aruba. It is the island nation's largest indoor baseball training facility, offering elite development to local players as well as international players from the United States and other countries. It was here, after spending sunup to sundown and sometimes into the evening hours working at the academy, that her passion for baseball took off. She even remembers thinking out loud to herself that she could be involved with baseball the rest of her life, a statement often made by those living out their passions.

Not one to let grass grow under her feet, she ended up interning with the historic Cape Cod Baseball League during her college years. The major league scouts attending these games took notice of this coach who was hitting fungoes, throwing BP, and coaching bases. That coach was a female. Kayla Baptista generated a lot of interest as the first female coach intern in the prestigious collegiate summer league's rich history. Her journey in the Cape Cod league adds to the narrative of women making strides in traditionally male-dominated sports roles. She expresses that her experience was, "absolutely unbelievable." You can sense a bit of emotion in her voice when she talks about what it meant to her. She thinks back and says that it was her first baseball experience and it could have made her or broken her. Fortunately, it did not break her; it propelled her. She classified that experience as literally living a dream.

There was more baseball work for Kayla at Cressey, a high-performance baseball and health training organization, in the 2021 and 2022 off-seasons. She continued with her UNC career, serving on their coaching staff, and finally graduating early. All of those experiences opened up more opportunities for her, including with the Texas Rangers.

The Rangers reached out to her to participate in what is called their coach identification program, which is nothing more than an on-field job interview. She joined the instructional league for the Rangers' minor leaguers in Arizona. In that job she ran live on-field practices, hit fungoes for fielding practice, and talked and lived baseball almost 24/7, including baseball philosophy, strategy, culture, team and player development. That on-field interview was successful, as the Rangers then offered her a job, making her feel honored to be part of a new wave of coaches in professional baseball. By this time, she had graduated from UNC and headed back to Arizona, working with Ranger players rehabbing from injuries. She ran batting practice as well as defensive skills practice with the men of her team. Yes, Kayla was part of the organization in her apprentice role when the Rangers won the World Series and yes, she did get a championship ring; quite an accomplishment at the age of twenty-two and maybe a preview of things to come.

Kayla was then hired as a player development coaching apprentice, making her the first female in the organization's history hired for a coaching role. Ranger management reported, "She is very qualified, passionate, very driven, and we as an organization value those things."

The amazing thing about this path is how quickly it all happened. Kayla is one to work hard, is many times relentless in moving toward her goals, and crams a lot into shorter periods of time than the average person. She graduated in three years from UNC with a four-year degree. She interned and coached while playing and coaching college softball and now she is rising quickly as a Texas Rangers coach. That's quite the path to follow for anyone wants to be involved in professional baseball, not only as a female but anyone with that dream.

At the time of this writing, Kayla was filling the role of a full-time player development coach for the Rangers. That mostly entails working with the Ranger Rookie League players, spending the whole baseball season at their developmental and spring training facility in Arizona. She works with infielders, coordinating practices for them as well as working with outfielders. She writes practice plans, executes the plans with the players, presents development plans, daily drills, and skills practice to them and coaches them along the way. She can even step in and coach first base while serving in any needed coaching position in rookie league management.

After her previous season she was involved in the post-season instructional league again coordinating infield and outfield players and practices. The Arizona Fall League followed this, and she stuck around on her own to help out. The Rangers AA manager was the manager of the Surprise Saguaros fall league team, giving her more exposure. After that she worked mostly with Ranger players going through rehabilitation from injuries, getting them back up to full time playing speed. At the time of this conversation, she was waiting for spring training to start. Her mindset is to immerse herself in anything baseball-related to help the team and the players, a true coach's mentality.

Baseball is Kayla's life. However, there are pros and cons to being the only female on the field. Starting out, she talks about players who approach her and seem more curious at first about working with a female. She mentions that this alone is a positive and shows that she is very approachable, an important coaching characteristic. This leads to them asking her questions, almost, she says, as if they are testing her knowledge and whether she has what it takes to be their coach. Once players realize she is a baseball person, knows what she is talking about, and is on a level keel with them from a baseball point of view, they grow to really like her. That, she says, makes for a great coach-player relationship where gender does not even come into play.

Also as a positive, players seem to grow to a point where they open up to her. Many players' mother figures are in another country and although Kayla is young, she is the female presence in their lives while they are with the team. Deep down she cares for her players, wants what is best for them, and does have a bit of a soft side but she can be tough on players when needed. Players realize that and know it is all part of the relationships that start, grow, and continue on the field. When talking with Kayla, there is a very positive air around her conversations about her on-the-field player relationships.

Just like anything else, there are negatives to talk about. The obvious factors are present. The female locker room (who she is the only one to use) is on the opposite side of the complex far away from the male coaching facilities. Coaches like to talk in the locker room, and since she is not there, she misses that. Coaches talk about the day's activities, the plans for the next day, and generally, as Kayla says, they bond there. She is not privy to those conversations. She compensates through what she calls creating her own space, letting players and coaches know they can approach her anywhere. It's not ideal but she says it works.

Gender issues never came up in her selection interviews. She is quick to point out that when she shows up on the field, she really doesn't feel different from any other coach. The Rangers are keen on hiring leaders who understand that everyone has something to contribute, all with a high level of respect. She gives credit to Ranger management for hiring the right people for that.

Gender does come up in media interviews. She doesn't like it but respects it and deals with it, as it goes with the territory. She admits it isn't easy. If it were easy, more women would be doing what she does. Other women have left the coaching ranks. Kayla says it takes a certain type of person to be a female coach in a man's world, and agrees it's still a man's world, but knows it will evolve.

Kayla winds up by emphasizing that she loves her work. Sure, there are issues with fitting into the clothes and uniforms offered, but she gets over that quickly. Missing family back home is tough, but she is managing.

There is a lot to learn from Kayla and all that she is doing. Younger females and even those her age or older can learn from her. When I asked her what advice she would give, she offered some very good guidance based on her experience, which is to, "Put yourself out there." Don't be afraid to reach out for what you want and don't be afraid to be rejected. It happens. Figure out how to engage with those that have influence over what you want. Sure, it will take more effort than it would for a male, but going after goals and facing rejection along the way shouldn't be viewed as a struggle. That sounds like common advice to anyone pursuing goals but it's what worked for Kayla and can work for others.

Kayla is proud of her resume of accomplishments and experience. She is often told that she has a strong background. She says she doesn't work to build a resume; the resume will come. That translates into another piece of advice for those up and coming: Let the resume build itself. Don't take jobs because they look good. The resume will build through your hard work and determination. Just let it happen.

Kayla has been strongly influenced by past coaches on her path. Early on, her travel softball coaches instilled in her, in a big way, the desire to dominate the fundamentals and to have precision in the detail of her work. She loved that process and it heavily impacted her game and her life beyond the game. Everything matters, which carries over to the philosophies of her current employer, the Texas Rangers. Core values for the Rangers are three-fold. Number one is to be a good teammate, followed by that principle of dominating the fundamentals. Core values wrap up with what she calls the third pillar, competing with passion. These values apply to all players, coaches, and employees of the Rangers organization.

Kayla remains unfazed by the world of professional baseball traditionally being male-dominated. Instead, she focuses on her passion for the game and the opportunities it presents. Luck may have played a part in her career, but it is evident that her success is primarily a result of her relentless efforts and commitment.

In a field where gender disparities persist, Kayla is not seeking special treatment. She has earned the respect of her peers, players, and fellow coaches through her hard work and dedication. Her presence in the baseball community serves as an inspiration and a symbol of the changing landscape within the sport. As more women like Kayla rise through the ranks, they contribute to breaking down barriers and challenging traditional norms in the world of professional baseball.

When talking to her about her future, whether with the Rangers or not, she puts it out there, while open to opportunities along the way. Her ultimate goal is to become the manager of a major league team. Sure, she knows there are obstacles to overcome. She also has an open mind and now that she has a few years' experience under her belt, she sees other roles that she may fulfill. Things like field coordinator, infield coordinator, or full director of player development could be future positions for her. At this point, being with the Texas Rangers for an extended time is her hopeful vision.

Kayla expressed in late 2023 heading into the following year, "Another season full of blessings as a Texas Ranger! Ready for what's next, 2024." Everyone wants someone with vigor, anticipation, and excitement. all while being appreciative and feeling blessed. That's Kayla Baptista.

Kayla Baptista is breaking barriers. Her success is opening doors for others and challenging the notion of coaching roles being exclusively for men.

Younger girls reaching out to learn more makes her smile. She sees on social media and listening in general that young girls are saying, "I never knew I could do this." She says, "I'm offering a vision that they can realize it is possible. I like being that influencer, providing positive energy and fueling the dreams of others."

The bottom line is that challenges still exist. The increasing number of women entering coaching roles in MLB indicates positive strides toward a more inclusive and diverse future for the sport. As more opportunities open up, women are making their mark and contributing to the growth and evolution of Major League Baseball.

Veronica Alvarez—A Visible Passion

Veronica Alvarez was recently named the Oakland Athletics' coordinator of player development in Latin America. Her focus is on operations and coaching at the team's Dominican Republic academy, where the A's send many of their prospects from all over Latin America.

People who visit Instagram often come upon her profile. With Instagram being the second most accessed social network, it's no surprise that her smiling face and friendly demeanor captivate a wide audience. With over one billion active monthly users and 500 million daily Instagram stories, it provides the perfect stage for Veronica to share her insights, coaching tips, and snippets of her life.

Everyone and their dog, literally, is on the social media platform, including Veronica's dog, Biggie Smalls.

"Everyone," includes individuals, pets, and, you guessed it, major league baseball coaches. Veronica stands out with her blend of personal and professional content. Among Veronica's regular features is "Mini Mic Monday," a candid Q&A video series where she introduces colleagues from USA Baseball, MLB, and her team, the Athletics. These videos provide viewers with insights into the lives of athletes, lessons learned from their experiences, and real-life baseball anecdotes. Through this series, Veronica not only showcases her connections within the baseball community but offers valuable advice and inspiration to her followers. Any of the videos will surely bring a smile to the face of those watching.

In addition to her advice and inspiration, she is serving as a beacon of encouragement and empowerment for aspiring female coaches, making strides toward a more diverse and inclusive future in baseball.

For those looking to get to know Veronica better, her Instagram feed serves as a window into her world, offering glimpses of her hobbies, her job, likes, dislikes, friends, family, and interactions with coworkers. Whether you're interested in baseball coaching, pet antics, or simply getting to know a friendly major league coach, Veronica's Instagram account promises to be an enjoyable visit for all.

Veronica is enthusiastic about leveraging social media and other platforms to provide visibility for baseball opportunities, particularly for the next generation. Her advice and the advice from her co-workers to the upcoming generation about hard work, seizing opportunities, and having

the courage to pursue their goals is valuable and empowering. Encouraging them to consistently put in effort and
take advantage of the chances that arise can certainly contribute to their personal and professional growth. That's
certainly one of Veronica's cornerstone pieces of advice.

It's fantastic to see Veronica Alvarez, a uniformed
coach, taking the initiative to share real-live coaching
on Instagram, especially for those interested in pursuing a
career in coaching professional baseball.

Alvarez's willingness to showcase her coaching expertise on a platform like Instagram is commendable, as it
helps break down barriers and encourages diversity in this
traditionally male-dominated realm. By sharing her experiences, tips, and insights, she contributes to the broader
community's understanding of the profession, fostering
inclusivity and opening doors for aspiring coaches.

This kind of visibility is crucial to promoting equal
opportunities in sports coaching and inspiring the
next generation of talent. It creates a positive ripple effect
by challenging stereotypes and showcasing the skills and
passion that make a successful coach, regardless of gender.

When studying women in baseball's leadership roles
it's always good to see the words, "…full-time role to head
up…" That's exactly how it was described when the Oakland A's announced Veronica Alvarez and her new full-
time position, after she had been a part-time instructor
in the A's organization for the past several years. She was
hired to improve the coordination of the A's Dominican
Republic team for Latin American prospects with their

minor league development complex in Arizona. Veronica's role is to develop and prepare Latino players for their eventual move to the U.S., " develop and prepare" being typical terms in a coach's job description.

As reported by Matt Kawahara in the *Houston Chronicle*, A's general manager David Forst said, "From a player development standpoint, the more we could align the two places the better."

The Athletics' Assistant GM Dan Feinstein said of Alvarez at the time of her hiring, "In my mind, she was the perfect fit for this position. She's extremely passionate. She has a ton of energy. She's knowledgeable. She has a way of relating to not only the players but the staff and coaches that are already in place in the Dominican." Gender did not enter into the decision or the comments.

Ed Sprague, director of A's player development, is the one who proposed hiring Alvarez to head up the revamping of the Dominican program. Sprague said of Veronica, "The biggest thing is the enthusiasm level Veronica brings and the passion she brings on a daily basis to that program."

Veronica stepped right into her new role after time with the U.S. National Women's team and prior experience with other softball and baseball teams. Her new role is her opportunity to help young players in the A's Dominican system bridge a cultural and geographical divide to further their baseball careers.

Her emphasis on education is a large part of bridging that gap. She supports the team's director of education in the Dominican Republic, helps players get their

GEDs, and pushes English classes for all of her players. She further emphasizes development for players to make their transition to United States baseball wise and culturally, easier, and better. She taps on her experience of living in both cultures as being the daughter of Cuban refugees/immigrants and her upbringing in the multi-cultural city of Miami.

Her role is enacting change and doing things in new ways, the Veronica Alvarez way. She is no stranger to enacting change, as one of a rising number of women who have landed roles in baseball leadership in recent years.

Alvarez became the first woman to manage a game in the A's system in 2022 for Oakland's High-A affiliate, the Lansing (Michigan) Lugnuts. She has also coached and managed in MLB-sponsored youth development programs focusing on girls' baseball. Alvarez proudly states, "If I can make an impact in these players' lives, and within the organization, that's what I want to do."

Veronica is aware of her impact and the impact of other female coaches in the game. She talks of how in just the past five to six years major league baseball has gotten to the point where she doesn't know how many female coaches there are. That's a sign of progress. She says it's no longer as much of a unique topic. It still is of interest, and she still wants to spread her messages, all in view of continuing progress.

In talking with people like Veronica and learning about their journey, the question of why she does what she does comes up. Veronica speaks clearly about her "why," which is very important to her.

In fact, it's important to all of us. Simon Sinek is a renowned author and inspirational speaker and author of the book *Start with Why*. He says, "Our whys are an articulation of who we are. For most, a good WHY statement is simple, easy to understand, and reflective of the person to whom it belongs. The WHY statement should not include WHATs (the tangible things we do/job titles/etc). It should embody who you are in every facet of your life, not just work."

Sinek explains that "Why" is probably the most important message an organization or individual can communicate because it inspires others to action. He further states, "Start with 'Why' is how you explain your purpose and the reason you exist and behave as you do." Veronica Alvarez embodies the purpose and reason of "Why."

In an older MLB article, Veronica was asked the very question of why she does what she is doing. As reported in *MLB Cut 4* regarding her "why," Veronica stated, "Obviously, I understand the role I'm playing. I'm trying to make a good impression. I'm trying to open the minds of men; I'm trying to show girls and women that you can accomplish everything. Those are my 'whys,' you know, what you talk about when someone asks why you do something. Why? For every little girl that has a dream to be involved in the game, to let them know that it's a possibility, that you just have to set your mind to it and work hard. And you know even women that never thought that this was a possibility but always wanted it, same thing."

Veronica Alvarez's journey in baseball is a testament to her resilience and determination in the face of adversity. Despite challenges, detours, and skeptics along the way, her passion for the sport and her sense of belonging on the baseball field have remained unwavering.

Being a woman in a male-dominated world has not deterred Alvarez; instead, it has fueled her commitment to breaking barriers. Her comfort on the baseball field is not just about being a player; it's a result of a lifetime dedicated to studying and understanding the intricacies of the game she loves.

As reported by usabaseball.com, Veronica says, "I'm a woman in this male-dominated world, but I honestly feel comfortable there. There's nowhere I'm more comfortable than on a baseball field."

Alvarez's comfort on the field comes naturally. She discovered her calling as a ballplayer early in life. Instead of the ballet classes suggested by her parents, she tagged along to her big brother's baseball games and included herself wherever she could. Her deep understanding of the game has been honed through years of play, dedicated study, practice, and performance.

Alvarez's story is a powerful example of following one's passion, regardless of societal norms or expectations. It speaks to the importance of believing in one's self, perseverance, and a genuine love for what you do. As she continues to navigate the challenges, Veronica Alvarez stands as an inspiration for others aspiring to overcome obstacles and pursue their dreams in any field, they are passionate about.

Veronica Alvarez's passion for the game of baseball is evident in every aspect of her involvement with the sport. Whether she's discussing her local baseball community in Miami, reminiscing about her time as a player and manager for USA Baseball's women's national team, or reflecting on her experiences during spring training with the Oakland Athletics, her enthusiasm is unmistakable. You can sure hear it when she talks of her current job with the Athletics.

This passion is not just a fleeting emotion for Alvarez; it's a constant presence that radiates through her expressions and resonates in her voice. As she engages in conversations about the intricacies of the game, her face lights up, and her voice carries a tone that reflects her deep connection with baseball.

Alvarez's passion extends beyond her personal experiences; it also encompasses the people who have been part of her journey. When she speaks about those she has learned from—whether they are colleagues she has worked alongside or played with, or formidable opponents on the field—her admiration and respect are evident. The impact of these individuals has contributed to her growth in the sport, and Alvarez acknowledges their role in shaping her understanding and love of baseball.

In essence, Veronica Alvarez is not just a participant in the world of baseball; she is a passionate advocate, a dedicated player, and a committed coach. Her love for the game transcends the boundaries of her roles, making her an inspiring figure for those around her in the baseball community and others that are watching her.

It seems that Veronica Alvarez is all over. She shows up in the media often and is the best commercial for women in baseball coaching. In an interview with Lauen Shehadi of MLB Central of the MLB Network, Alvarez told her, "Girls belong in baseball. That's why I try to get in people's eyes and cameras. That why I do what I do." Keep an eye out for her. She's going places.

Veronica Alvarez's merits continue on her baseball path. She now adds the title of "beacon" to her trailblazing resume. At the time of this writing in mid-March 2024, Veronica Alvarez was named MLB's first Girls Baseball Ambassador. Veronica is proud that she has been an integral part of MLB's Girls Baseball Development programs since their inception.

Veronica is dedicated to making space and time for the next generation of women in baseball and softball, because she knows how essential that level of guidance and care is for someone's journey. Veronica will use her new role to take her passion for providing opportunities for women and girls in the sport to another level.

"Veronica has been a valuable presence alongside our efforts to grow the game among women and girls," said Tony Reagins, MLB's chief baseball development officer. "Her achievements as a player, manager, professional coach and in player development will inspire young women to not only play our game but also pursue their own successes at the highest levels. We are excited to continue this journey with her."

There is a lot more to Veronica's journey and past, but it is clear that her journey will lead her to higher levels and greater success.

Katie Krall—A Remarkable Path

Who gets a history degree from one of the country's leading private research and teaching universities and gets their first job upon graduation in baseball? Who, today, is still working in baseball, including major league coaching? Katie Krall is that person and her baseball path is remarkable.

MLB appreciates the praise and accolades that come with hiring Rachel Balkovec, Kim Ng and other trailblazers, but the sport still has a long way to go to fix its representation problem. The hiring of Katie Krall is part of that fix.

Katie's baseball fire goes back to the days when her mother pulled her and her twin sister out of school to go to a Chicago White Sox or Chicago Cubs game. It was during these games that her mom taught her how to keep score. As a ten-year-old, she regularly questioned her coach about lineup composition. That coach was Katie's dad.

Her passion for the sport grew further when she attended the 2003 All-Star Game at U.S. Cellular Field, in Chicago. It wasn't until she read *Moneyball* that Krall realized she could challenge the convention of male domination of the sport. From that point on, it became clear that a career in baseball was Katie's goal and aspiration.

Today Katie Krall is a former development coach in the Boston Red Sox organization, serving as the Portland (Maine) Sea Dogs affiliate's development coach, where she integrated new technology and data into advance scouting, in-game strategy, and player plans to improve on-field performance. She also collaborated with the baseball analytics and sports science departments to construct goals for players as they relate to run creation and run prevention based on quantitative metrics. Prior to her Red Sox role, she worked as a baseball operations analyst for the Cincinnati Reds. She gained more baseball experience in her job at the Office of the Commissioner of Major League Baseball. Within a short time, she even worked as an assistant general manager in the Cape Cod league. Between stints, she planned the World Series Trophy Tour for the Cubs in 2016. Katie Krall was and is definitely a baseball girl.

In her role as the Red Sox operations analyst, Katie developed tools to improve decision-making processes for roster construction, game planning, and R & D, in addition to providing pro scouting coverage. She was also involved in roster construction, trade decisions and draft selections, which was described as a role not unlike Jonah Hill's in the film version of *Moneyball*.

Katie's experience with the Office of the Commissioner was serving as the first female diversity and inclusion fellow at the sports headquarters. When asked about this job, Katie stated in an interview for an LPGA women's networking publication, "It was really powerful to be at the central hub of baseball and to be part of something that combined my two loves of baseball and promoting gender equality."

She had since graduated from Northwestern University, where she played on the golf team. Now, what about that history degree? Not to worry: with that degree in her pocket, she pursued her MBA from the University of Chicago and is at the time of this writing an adjunct professor at Northwestern in the Masters of Sports Administration Program, in addition to her baseball duties.

Katie, the first woman to coach at the Double-A level, is a career baseball girl and just getting started. She is now the Senior Product Manager of global baseball strategy for Hawkeye, a UK-based technology company working with MLB that fuels analytics for the teams. In this role she continues to look at technological advances and team expectations for the next decade and beyond. When discussing Hawkeye and Katie's work, you hear terms like biomechanics data, injury prevention, return-to-play data, and more. It has been said that Katie's position with Hawkeye represents a natural outgrowth of her ability to distill and analyze data and make it relevant at the player, coach, and executive levels. For her, as she says, it's an opportunity to be in the trenches of biomechanics data, which she thinks is the next frontier in baseball on the hitting and pitching side.

Katie left her team coaching job for a role in which she is still very much involved in baseball, just in a different capacity. Katie stated in that same LPGA publication, highlighting her post-golf, post-Northwestern time, "I possess a restlessness to do more. So, whether that's graduating from Northwestern in three years, completing my MBA from the University of Chicago in less than two, I think there is this need to climb the next mountain."

While Katie Krall broke ground and was a "first" in coaching, she is quick to say, "I've noticed there is a generation of women who have seen Alyssa Nakken with the Giants, who have seen Bianca Smith with the Red Sox, that being a female coach isn't necessarily inconceivable anymore, so I hope that they build on what we're currently doing right now. We're getting to a place where I guess this is normal. It's not, 'you're a female baseball coach' or 'you're a female hockey coach.' You're a coach. In the same way that you're not a 'female lawyer' or a 'female doctor.' You're a doctor and you're a lawyer."

Katie, like all other women coaches interviewed, is a fierce advocate for women in baseball coaching and the front office. She subscribes to the Selig principle as told by a mentor of hers, Wendy Selig-Prieb, who served for six years as CEO of the Milwaukee Brewers, the franchise once owned by her father and a former MLB commissioner. That principle is that as a person rises, they should use both hands: one to reach up and grab for more and lead and the other to reach down and pull others up. Katie has been proactive in helping other women find jobs in baseball as best she can. She advises any and all to know exactly what they want and be proactive in seeking interviews. The recent upward trend of women hired in baseball has happened as a result of some of the advice and practical steps Katie speaks of. Women are very qualified for jobs in MLB. Opening doors for them will also open doors for those who come later.

When the subject of advocacy comes up, Katie says it's so powerful to have women on the field, powerful for representation, and powerful for boys and girls seeing women on the field even if they don't want to work in baseball. Seeing a coach with a ponytail (implying a female ponytail) is a definite paradigm shift for all involved including fans. Katie goes on to say, "That paradigm shift is normalizing what was once impossible."

Katie says that the aim is for normalization of women in baseball. She says it will be incredibly meaningful when the day arrives that her story and path aren't an anomaly. Her goal, like that of all the other women coaches talked to, is to be seen simply as someone pursuing their dream.

She is proud to say that during her time coaching for the Red Sox affiliate, the players and coaches were very respectful. She said that's what made that whole experience worthwhile. That is increasingly the case as more females enter MLB coaching roles. She also says with pride that it's important to her that young girls and other women see someone at first base, coaching, with a ponytail. Also, during her time with the Sea Dogs, right after a game she encountered two younger women who exclaimed, "We are women in sports too. We work at ESPN and think it's so amazing that you're here in the dugout." This prompted to Katie to once again realize the importance of women in professional baseball. She said that moment was bigger than baseball. The fact that she can coach first base, and a little girl watching might say, "Hey, wait a minute, who's that out there? Maybe I can do that," she considers extraordinary.

In Katie's own interview of Janet Marie Smith, who was executive vice president of planning and development for the Los Angeles Dodgers, she said some of the most successful companies are headed up by women, so why not baseball? Smith went on to say, "We see a lot more women playing sports and I think Title IX did everything we hoped it would do when it passed. It's not nearly as foreign an idea as it was a generation ago to have women in sports."

Katie was asked about advice for those wanting to get in the game. She summed it up by saying that the impossible is now a construct, that if someone brings the skills that aid in development and success, there is a place for that person in MLB. She went on to advise that for every one person saying females working in baseball is not possible today, there are two people saying yes, it is possible and to go for it. That two-to-one ratio has grown and will get better as time goes forward and the current female in baseball trend continues.

More advice came forth in a conversation with Katie. She says tenacity is paramount, or as the Oxford dictionary defines it, "the quality or fact of being very determined." Anyone wanting to break into baseball coaching and the MLB must be very determined to do so.

Katie urges other women to be strategic and intentional with efforts to go forward in applying, interviewing, networking, and showing up to be seen. Education is just as important. Those looking at resumes look at educational credentials as well as anything and everything related to baseball specific experience.

Opportunities for women in professional baseball, like Katie Krall has shown, have been growing rapidly. In a social media post she said, "Ever since I was a little girl, I have wanted to leave my mark on the history of baseball. It's an honor and privilege to continue to be part of this industry as more incredible women write the next chapter of the game's story."

Katie confirmed that it is absolutely her intention to be back with an MLB team either in uniform as a coach or as part of the front office. She said she absolutely wants to help an organization win championships.

Katie's real wish is to be in uniform acting as a conduit between the front office and staff on the field. This role could revolve around optimizing hitting, pitch design, and in-game strategy, a job that Katie says must exist for a team to be more successful. It could take the form of becoming an advance scouting coach or something new. Being in uniform is like an infield coach being in uniform; it emphasizes the strategic and tactical importance to players and other coaches and is welcoming for players approaching the person in that position. It lends credibility to the role she is suggesting and wanting.

Along those same lines, Katie told the *Boston Globe* early in her Red Sox career, "Once you get a taste of it, once it's in your blood, nothing can compare to it. As arduous as the grind can be, there's something extraordinary about being part of the day-to-day cadence where you have a chance to win every night and to help other players." Katie has had that taste and will return. She states loud and clear that she wants to be a difference maker.

Bianca Smith—Pivoting with An International Twist

Bianca Smith is at a point in her baseball career where she clearly is pivoting. Psychologically, the word "pivot" refers to the process of taking things to a new place. Pundits describe the pivot mindset as one that is anchored in a clear and confident vision, continually evolving based on past experiences while not being limited by them. A pivoting mindset embraces feedback and experience, allowing it to shape the vision into something greater. That describes Bianca Smith and all that she is doing.

What is she pivoting from and how is she accomplishing this? Let's take a look.

During the 2021 season, Bianca Smith became the first Black woman to serve as a professional baseball coach, working as a minor league coach in the Red Sox organization. Part of her role is helping players at the team's spring facility perfect their swings and pitch accuracy. It truly was an on-the-field job and experience.

Bianca gives a lot of baseball inspiration credit to her late mother, who died of cancer in 2013 after igniting her passion for baseball. Smith recalled many memories of watching her mother cheering for her favorite team, the New York Yankees. We won't even discuss what her Yankees fan mother would think of Bianca's employment with the rival Red Sox.

Bianca was actually interested in watching baseball before playing it. Her youth sports experience revolved around soccer. She then moved into softball, the typical female path, even though her knowledge and desire still centered around baseball. At the time, females weren't involved with baseball. Not until she joined the first club baseball team at her alma mater, Dartmouth College, did she actually play with a higher-level team. She started every game in right field and batted second, which was quite a formidable record for a female in baseball.

Her interest in baseball was solid then, solid prior to that, and is solid now. Her initial interest was baseball operations with a target of Major League Baseball general management. Her idea was to work where she would have an impact on the roster and game performance of a team, which is where she thought the front office path would lead. She even went to graduate school, seeking two degrees, to learn management, legal fundamentals, and more to help with this goal.

She pursued that path, tried it and after two operations internships she discovered that she didn't want to be in the front office and it wasn't the way to fulfill her true desires. She quickly concluded she wanted to be on the field in a coaching, training, and development capacity. She felt that was the path to the roster impact and game performance influence she wanted most. She still didn't see many, if any, women coaching. However, her parents raised her to realize that when it comes to something you want and you are driven, gender shouldn't matter. That lesson and attitude propelled Bianca to higher heights.

In an article on Newsone.com, a site that bills itself as a destination for news and information for and about African Americans, it was reported that her internship with the Cincinnati Reds in 2019 was a turning point. That was when she decided coaching, not front-office work, was her real calling. Finally, she had found what she loved and wanted to do in baseball. She'd be a manager in the dugout, not a general manager at a desk.

The article went on to say that in Bianca's downtime in the baseball operations department, she watched practice from the stands and took notes.

She told Donnie Ecker, then an assistant hitting coach, that she was interested in coaching. He offered to help on the field, and Reds manager David Bell encouraged her to bring her glove to practice.

By the end of her internship, Smith was helping at practices by catching throws and warming up the coaches and players, and on game days was in the clubhouse analyzing hitters' swing decisions. Every day, she made sure to ask coaches at least one meaningful question about baseball, as they were interested in her thoughts.

Bell said, "Bianca could walk into a major league staff right now and contribute? No doubt. I really believe that she is capable of doing anything in this game."

In 2022, Smith was back coaching for the Red Sox at their Fort Myers, Florida development complex and subsequently coached for the Scottsdale Scorpions in the Arizona Fall League. However, despite having a multi-year offer on the table, Smith left the Red Sox organization in 2023 to seek a new opportunity.

Smith explained that she didn't feel challenged enough in her role. The Red Sox wanted her to manage the rookie ball team, but because of her passion for game strategy and management, she declined. That's when she started her pivot. She had her goals and values in mind and continued to move more toward them.

"They wanted to send me back to rookie ball and I had no desire to be there, so I decided to take my chance," Smith said in an interview with *The Athletic*. "My passion is (game) strategy and rookie ball is almost entirely player development."

Smith is not giving up on a dream of returning to MLB; she's simply taking a different path. Last summer, this baseball fanatic relocated to Japan, where she is coaching elementary and middle school baseball through the JET (Japanese Exchange and Teaching) program—a long-standing item on her baseball "bucket list." Additionally, Smith has taken on a new coaching role with the Great Britain women's national baseball team and the British

23-and-under team. Dividing her time is a whole other story. For now, we will leave it as, "baseball to the max."

In the current Japanese phase of her coaching career, Smith aims to be a sponge, absorbing as much information and as many diverse experiences as possible. She is particularly passionate about defensive strategies and baserunning, aspects of baseball that are more prominent in Japan. In fact, she recently shared with her social media audience: "If you've ever seen a Japanese youth baseball team, you've seen their synchronized running and shouting. They start practicing that in kindergarten. Seriously, we spend ten or fifteen minutes at the start of practice working on staying in sync and shouting while running."

Her initial emphasis in Japan was to teach English in addition to coaching. Although many coaches are involved in this effort, she found she was the only baseball coach and the only coach from America to do so.

With the influx of Nippon Professional Baseball (NPB) players coming to the U.S., there are very few coaches to work with and help the Asian players while speaking their language and understanding their culture. Bianca's desire and goal is to bridge that gap and fill that void in MLB.

She is now coaching and developing players in elementary and middle school baseball in Hokkaido in northern Japan. She classifies her job as something she wanted, something she likes, and something that represents a steppingstone to furthering her baseball career. Bianca clearly expresses that she wants to coach professional baseball in Japan. What she is doing now is networking, which allows her to learn the culture of Japan and Japanese base-ball. This experience will help in her professional pursuit, whether in Japan or the U.S. She has a clear goal of coach-ing professionally in Japan, perhaps within a couple of years. Beyond going pro in Japan is a desire to go pro in the U.S. major leagues beyond what she did with Boston Red Sox (unless, honestly, the right offer at the right time for the right amount of money comes in Japan).

When the subjects of gender, gender issues and gender challenges come up, Bianca thinks back to her steps along her baseball path, especially her upbringing. Whether or not her parents had foresight into her baseball career, they raised her to believe there are no gender roadblocks when pursuing goals and dreams.

When she started playing with her male counterparts, she thought to herself that there weren't other females playing. When she was asked about her interest in coach-ing at the major league level, she was hesitant because female coaches were not visible to her. She did want to coach though, and didn't let the lack of females stop her.

When she was initially announced as the first Black woman to be named as a major league coach, she was over-whelmed by the attention. She reflected, "I didn't appreci-ate the opportunity of that attention. I grew up with the belief that coaches should be behind the scenes, but now I do wish I had done more with it and used it as a platform." However, when she left her position with the Red Sox, she got even more attention. It wasn't just about her departure from professional baseball in the U.S.; it was about the departure of the only African American woman in that role. She found this spotlight uncomfortable, lamenting the lack of representation for Black girls to look up to in the profession.

Bianca Smith was featured in an article in *The Call to Lead*, a Dartmouth College community aimed at engaging with the significant issues of this and the next century. In the article, she was asked, "How has your experience as a woman in a male-dominated sport affected you?" Her response was candid: "I've never really thought about it. I've been a baseball fan since I can remember, probably since I was three or four years old. I never saw it as a male or female sport. People just play baseball. I credit my parents for that because they never emphasized gender roles. I've always approached every job as, 'Yes, I'm a woman who works in baseball. There's nothing else that needs to be said.'"

Fortunately, no gender questions came up during any of her interviews for baseball coaching. There may have been a subtle mention or two but she says she was oblivious to them. To put it bluntly, they weren't anything worth caring about. She focuses on doing her job, not gender. That's much the same as many others in her position these days. Baseball has evolved to that point and for that she is glad.

As she stated in her interview with *The Athletic*, "Looking back, I do believe I would have had more of a chance to advance if I wasn't a woman in the game. There could have been things behind the scenes that I didn't know about. But every industry has issues like that to deal with. As far as on the baseball field, I didn't have any issues and still don't."

When asked about promoting diversity, Bianca candidly admits she could and wants to do more. She consistently mentions diversity and inclusion in all her interviews and now aims to use that platform more effectively, to emphasize the need for avenues for women to coach in men's baseball, particularly at the professional level. She points out that in Japan, where the culture and tradition dictate that coaches and managers are usually former players, there are few women who are qualified to work in men's leagues. With the increasing popularity of women's baseball in Japan, there should be more opportunities for female coaches to join men's teams. Those opportunities are not abundant now, but they are coming.

Bianca Smith, the trailblazing first Black woman to coach professional baseball, is setting a unique example with an international flair. Her pivoting is allowing her to shape her vision into something greater. Her multicultural background, combined with her innate drive and unwavering passion for excellence in her sport, sets her apart.

Justine Siegal—Relentless Pursuit of Gender Equity

From the *Christian Science Monitor*:

> "Justine Siegal had been passionate about baseball since her days in Little League.

She often slept with one hand gripped on her bat in case she wanted to practice swings in the middle of the night. She played third base and pitched on her all-boys high school team. Her dream was always to take the field for the Cleveland Indians. But as she grew older and the reality set in that there was no pathway for a woman to become a professional ballplayer, she refocused. Her new goal: become a coach."

Justine Siegal was raised in a family of what could be considered baseball fanatics. She wanted to play baseball, not softball, at her private high school in the Cleveland, Ohio area but was not allowed to set foot at the team try-outs. After that refusal, she enrolled in a local baseball camp where she ended up pitching against some of her classmates. The early result was that she struck out batter after batter, retiring the side in more than one game. At that point, those involved knew she was changing their minds and the minds of those who refused her participation because of her gender.

Justine Siegal is a former Major League Baseball coach, a sports educator, and the founder of Baseball for All. She became the first female coach of a professional men's team when she worked for the Brockton (Massachusetts) Rox in the independent Canadian American Association of Professional Baseball. In 2011, she became the first woman to throw batting practice to an MLB team, the Cleveland

Indians (now the Guardians). She has also thrown batting practice to the Tampa Bay Rays, St. Louis Cardinals, Houston Astros, and New York Mets. In 2015, when hired by the Oakland Athletics for their instructional league in Arizona, she became the first female coach employed by an MLB team.

Siegal, with her passion, participation and advocacy, is interested and active in promoting sports gender equity.

When a coach told the thirteen-year-old Siegal she couldn't play baseball anymore even though she was one of the best players in the league, she didn't listen. The coach's only reason for the denial was gender. In fact, he bluntly stated, "I don't want you on my team, girls should play softball."

Even at that age, Siegal was not one to give up. She found ways to stick with her favorite sport, and later, after earning her PhD in sports and exercise psychology, she went on to her trailblazing professional coaching career.

We understand her path into baseball and the driving forces behind her passions. When asked about her entry into coaching, Justine reflected on her journey, saying coaching has always been her aspiration. Despite facing ridicule, laughter, and dismissive comments that no man would ever listen to a woman on the baseball field, she persevered, growing increasingly determined to achieve her dream. Starting by coaching at baseball camps, she progressed to college baseball, and ultimately the professional realm. Her journey began with a goal, a fervent passion, and an unwavering and relentless pursuit of her true desires.

I inquired about Justine's move into professional coaching with the Brockton Rox and how she secured that role. True to her style, Justine stressed that she wasn't just chosen or simply selected. She worked diligently, displayed her qualifications, and leveraged her network. With her background in college coaching and impressive credentials, she discovered an opportunity. Attending a SABR meeting, she crossed paths with Mike Veeck, son of perennial baseball executive Bill Veeck. Mike Veeck's career has included work with a wide variety of teams from both the affiliated and independent ranks (like the St. Paul Saints, Charleston RiverDogs, and the Rox). Following numerous interviews, she was hired for the coaching position with the Rox.

Besides her minor-league coaching experience and her PhD, Siegal's qualifications include completion of the Major League Scouting Bureau's scout school, and playing, watching, and being part of baseball from early on.

Justine is now using her platform to advocate and give back to the next generation through Baseball for All, a nonprofit aimed at offering all girls opportunities to play, coach, and lead in baseball.

When asked what she is currently involved in, she said plainly that besides the all-encompassing duties of running and promoting Baseball for All, that she founded, she is busy with Baseball United as a first base coach for one of their new teams.

Baseball United, a professional league in the Middle East and South Asia, believes baseball will be the next great sport for the Mideast and India. The organization has the stated mission of inspiring one billion new fans to fall in love with baseball. Justine is on the ground floor of that effort and part of its early success. At the time of our chat and this writing, Justine was fresh off a week of coaching for Baseball United in Dubai.

Justine says of Baseball United, "We are building something beautiful here; not for us but for all the kids in this region who are now going to fall in love with baseball just like we did." It truly is a unique opportunity to engage youth athletes and others from the world's largest populations. That's just one more example of Justine Siegal's pioneering effort for her sport.

Elizabeth Benn, former MLB senior coordinator of player programs for baseball development and diversity, and at the time of this writing director of major league operations for the New York Mets, said, "She has blazed a trail for many women in baseball. The work she has done allowed doors to open for others. There are a lot of women coming up through the ranks at all levels including professional baseball now. Justine planted the seed." Justine modestly acknowledges her contribution to history but stresses that it's more important to build a better future for all young girls and women. Justine says, "I want girls to know they can follow their passions. That they have no limits, and that their dreams matter."

Justine Siegal is considered by many an amazing visionary, change agent, and women's inclusion champion.

From Justine's founder's message on the Baseball for All website:

"I was 13 years old the first time I was told I shouldn't play baseball because I was a girl.

My coach explained to me that he didn't want me on his baseball team and that I should play softball instead. It didn't matter that I was one of the best players on the team, that I loved baseball, or that I practiced way more than any of my male friends. It only mattered that I was a girl.

The day my coach told me to quit was the day I decided to play baseball forever.

Too many girls are still told they can't play baseball because they are girls. I founded Baseball for All to empower girls to believe in themselves and to keep playing the game they love. I fear if you tell a girl she can't play baseball what else will she think she can't do? I then worry what else boys will think girls can't do?

Baseball For All is leveling the playing field for girls across America by addressing the social justice issue of gender inequality. I want girls to know they can follow their passions. That they have no limits. That their dreams matter.

Together, we will show our girls that we be- lieve in them and their baseball dreams."

Up2Us Sports (Up2us.org) an organization with a mission to engage, train, and support coaches to transform youth, programs, and communities, asked Siegal a series of questions. Her replies are poignant and consistent with other advocates of women in MLB coaching.

When asked why it is so important to have more female coaches Justine replied, "This is a huge question with a lot of layers. But at its basic level, it's important to have female coaches in men's programming because we bring a diverse perspective. The coaching staff is stronger when diversity exists. If every coach knows the same thing and comes from basically the same background, then there is the risk of a stale staff. It's also important that girls and women realize that these jobs are open for them; that they know they are not judged by their gender but by what they can bring to the team. I think that's what all coaches want—to be seen for who they are and how they can con- tribute to the team."

When I posed the same question to Justine, she emphasized that diversity is a crucial factor in team suc- cess. Diversity simply helps teams win. By having qualified women on the field, teams can reach more players using traditional and innovative methods. In today's world, it's simply good business to have women coaches. Justine believes that baseball, being the greatest game, should be accessible to everyone, regardless of gender. This belief is at the core of Baseball for All. Initially, baseball was seen as a man's game, where women were filtered out. Justine advocates to ensure that women are no longer excluded.

Siegal was asked about advice for women and girls who run into gender issues, challenges and even doubters, on and off the field. Justine says to just keep going strong. No one can control how people treat others. Responses can be controlled. That's the attitude Siegal adopted early on. Her goal wasn't to be liked but to maintain her passion for the sport and keep moving inclusion forward. She recommends a high degree of focus and not letting the detractors interfere with that focus.

When asked about her advice for young women pursuing the sport, Justine admitted that her advice has evolved over the years. Initially, including from her own experience, she advised others to become overqualified and to maintain relentless focus and drive.

Today, her advice has become more specific, and she emphasizes that it applies equally to young men and women. Justine advises aspiring coaches to gain experience and acquire extensive knowledge of biomechanics. Additionally, she suggests learning Spanish, considering the increasing number of Latin American players in the league. Justine also stresses the importance of building and utilizing a network of connections, one of whom might know the person who can open the door to a valuable opportunity.

When Justine embarked on her journey, there was no established pathway or blueprint for becoming a major league coach. Now, she observes that welcoming pathways have emerged, particularly as more women enter the ranks. While she acknowledges significant progress, she also believes there is still a long way to go.

Facing gender-related challenges and potential obstacles was a familiar experience for Justine. She explains that whether as a player or a coach, she often found herself in the position of being either the only woman or the first woman in various endeavors. She describes her journey as that of an outsider, a situation she willingly placed herself in as part of her pursuit. Throughout it all, she remained steadfast in not allowing anything to hinder her progress.

During her time as a coach in the instructional league for the Oakland Athletics, Justine persistently emailed Billy Beane, the decision-maker on coaching matters, highlighting her playing time and educational background. She chose early on to study sport psychology and exercise psychology to complement her playing background. This approach proved successful, ultimately leading her to work for Beane. Interestingly, gender was never a topic of discussion in this context.

Notably, throughout all of Justine's pioneering efforts, her approach has been twofold. Her primary pursuit was for her own advancement, but she was also mindful of clearing the way for future female coaches. This dual purpose epitomizes the essence of a trailblazer, a title that could easily be Justine Siegal's middle name. She further notes that females in professional baseball have never been in a better position.

Someone like Justine is a believer in relentlessly continuing her mission of achieving gender equity in baseball. Her slant on doing more means finding ways to gain resources and support, just like male leagues and male players receive. It all boils down to allowing girls and women to blossom, as she says, into what they want to be. Part of her message and mission is getting these females to believe in themselves. While that is easier said than done, allocating resources and removing obstacles is her ongoing goal. She is specific and focused, even in small ways, to contribute to that cause.

Justine Siegal's vision for the future is a world where no girl ever has to hear that she is not allowed to be part of the sport because of her gender.

One of Justine Siegal's famous quotes is, "Let your kids play. Tell them you love watching them play and don't be their coach in the car on the way home." Her other message foundation is, "If you tell a girl she can't play baseball, what else will she think she can't do."

This trailblazer is all about baseball for all, much like her non-profit group's name suggests.

Alyssa Nakken—Trailblazer Extraordinaire

A trailblazer is a person who's the first to do something, whether it's marking a new path through the woods, discovering a cure for cancer, or being the first in sports to hold a particular position. Alyssa Nakken is a trailblazer. She is the first uniformed female full-time staff member as part of a coaching staff in the major leagues, the first woman to coach on the field in a major league game, the first woman to interview for an MLB managerial job, and now MLB's first coaching mom. At first, trailblazers shake up the sports landscape but then they start to shape it. That's Alyssa Nakken.

Nakken was a three-time all-conference softball player and four-time Academic All-American at Sacramento State. She earned her master's degree in sports management at the University of San Francisco and began her career with the San Francisco Giants in 2014 as a baseball operations intern.

At the time of this writing, Bob Melvin manages the Giants, having taken over recently from Gabe Kapler. Melvin has stated publicly that he is pleased to have inherited Nakken from Kapler's coaching staff. Nakken's title is still, "assistant major-league coach." Her duties are similar to those of then-new bench coach Ryan Christenson, assisting with the outfielders and baserunners and helping to map out spring training plans. She also assists with batting practice and manages the batting cage during games. Another important role she carries out is helping to on-board Melvin and his new staff. Right before she became baseball's first mom, she was considered a driving force for a coaches summit at the Arizona team facility to help with that process.

Manager Melvin describes her as a great resource, especially for the new players, as she helps to make them feel comfortable, explains how things are done, and puts them in touch with the right people. Melvin simply says, "She's on everything."

As far as being baseball's first mom, Giants general manager Pete Putila said, "That'll be a new experience for baseball, and we're excited to support her through that."

Nakken's first role in San Francisco's organization in 2014 was as an intern, which led to working in event logistics, business development, and coordinating health and wellness initiatives. Nakken then became one of Kapler's coaches, focused on things like in-game planning, baserunning, and outfield instruction.

Nakken's debut as the first female on-field coach wasn't exactly planned. During a Giants-Padres game, Giants first-base coach Antoan Richardson was ejected by the umpiring crew chief during a play dispute. Nakken was camped out near the batting cages, enjoying the game and performing her off-field coaching duties. Upon Richardson's ejection, fellow bench coach Kai Correa ran down to the cages and grabbed Nakken to insert her into the game as Richardson's replacement. Boom! History was made. One of the Giants' infielders, and I'm sure other players, recognized the move as a general replacement, stating "She is just one of us, but it was pretty cool to see her out there." As she told MLB, "Our first-base coach got thrown out. I've been training as a first-base coach for the last few years. I work alongside Antoan so I stepped into what I was hired to do."

In the same report by Maria Guardado, Giants beat writer for MLB, Nakken stated, "Everybody can just see that there are a lot of opportunities in baseball. Sometimes I think we always limit ourselves to thinking what we could do. At least that's my experience. I never thought that I could do something like this because I never saw it. So, I think, sure, it's certainly important for people to be able to see that this is an opportunity, and they can see somebody that kind of looks like them going out there and coaching in the big leagues."

When someone reaches a pinnacle or trailblazes, they often are asked for advice. Many young girls, women, and others see Alyssa Nakken and have many reactions. One is, "I didn't know women could do that." Another is, "How did she get there; what advice could she give me to do the same or something similar?"

Her advice is first, her example; what she is doing right now. She though, does offer other words of wisdom. Some are related to chasing a passion and other advice is more tactical in nature.

Tactically, she recommends that people should set a routine, whether related to health, meditation, workouts, exercise, or anything. This will allow those who do so to stay on track toward their goals. This includes setting aside time to be with family or to enjoy a hobby. Working toward or in a career can be overwhelming but having a routine that can be controlled is a foundation for all.

Secondly, she emphasizes an individual's network. A network is key when building and working in a career. It truly is a case of who you know. Thirdly, and she practiced this during her operations internship, is to not get stuck in a box. Don't get boxed in regardless of the job or industry or what has been done in the past. This really is a way of saying step out of the box in thinking and action. She is also quick to say, "Don't fall victim to labels." It all boils down to pursuing what one desires on a day-to-day basis without chasing titles, being first, or having the fastest or biggest of something. She says to chase what brings joy every day and make sure that joy appeals to a person's values. Gender doesn't matter here.

She further says to hunt for confidence in what a person does and stands for, every day. A person who lacks confidence can gain it by focusing on things that build a greater threshold of confidence. Attack those items, face the challenging moments, and keep going after them or building on them. Typically, anticipation gets in the way of confidence. Building confidence is a slow process but it will build as one walks into it, faces it, and walks through it.

She also practices learning something new every day. She did that as a Division 1 college softball player and is doing it now. When working initially with the Giants, she wanted to always learn more and get better. She did that and was then offered more opportunity. "Never stop learning," is her message loud and clear.

Alyssa practices most of that now. She continually tries to figure out and stay true to who she really is while making the biggest impact she can on her clubhouse, players, fellow coaches, staff, and fans.

Alyssa Nakken understands the spotlight she is in, the historical nature of her achievement, and states that she knows the responsibility that comes with being a trail-blazer, soon to be more of an icon. From day one with the Giants, Nakken embraced the part of her role as an opportunity to be an example for girls and women, show-ing them they can do anything they want if they put their minds to it.

Nakken has been quoted as saying, "I think we're all inspirations doing everything that we do on a day-to-day basis, and I think, yes, this carries a little bit more weight because of the visibility. Obviously, there's a historical nature to it, but this is my job."

Alyssa credits her success to her willingness to embrace any role and excel, especially in a career where she knows thousands would trade places with her in an instant. Alyssa modestly says she never thought she would be a coach but was looking forward to showing young girls and other women they too could land a spot in Major League Baseball.

She recently witnessed a young dad say to her during an autograph moment for his young daughter, "This is a girl dad home run. Thank you!" Another admirer, an older woman, told her, "I'm a seventy-year-old woman and was never able to play sports. My granddaughter can now see what is possible and what she can do."

Little girls, teenage girls, and other young women need to physically see a woman working on the field and in coaching positions like Alyssa Nakken's. For this reason, it is especially important that Alyssa shows up in the dugout.

Alyssa Nakken and her fellow coach and mentor Antoan Richardson have many heart-to-heart conversations. Richardson told Nakken early in her path that she wasn't ready for more coaching. She took this message to heart and both her and Richardson got back to work to focus even harder on things she didn't know. Alyssa's advice from all of this is to know what you don't know, which continues to be the case as she employs her learning attitude.

A coach is only as effective as the players are receptive to their coaching—no matter their gender, race, or anything else. What the Giants players show, day in and day out, is that they will take all the help they can get from whoever can provide it, male or female. Early on in her coaching Alyssa shared with new and veteran players her patented handshakes for some of the players she coached. You see these all the time between players (and coaches) after an at bat, a run scoring, or a celebratory event. Alyssa Nakken is not to be left out of these. That's just another indicator of her team's acceptance of her role just as a coach, not as a male or female.

In 2022 the Giants had a limited-edition Alyssa Nakken jersey giveaway for a specially ticketed Girls Night event. Then-pitching coach Andrew Bailey went for one of those jerseys for his daughters and said, "What she's done for our game has been phenomenal, and the acceptance she's gained as a woman on a big-league staff has been stellar. You see all these superstar athletes walk by and everyone in the crowd wants her attention. To touch the game like that is really special."

At the end of the day Alyssa Nakken is a baseball coach, not a female baseball coach. Her former manager and the one who hired her, Gabe Kapler, stated, "I think I would say it, I think our players would say it, I think our coaching staff would say that she's been just an extraordinary addition to our clubhouse and to the field when she's on it and to our staff in general, she made us a better baseball team."

Rachel Balkovec—Relentless and Fiery

"Major League Baseball is committed to pursue our sports as players, coaches, umpires, and executives." That was a statement by Commissioner of Baseball Rob Manfred in the announcement of Rachel Balkovec becoming the manager of the Tampa Tarpons, a single-A minor league affiliate of the New York Yankees in January 2022.

In January 2024, Rachel Balkovec was named the Miami Marlins' director of player development.

In talking with many of the women in MLB leadership and coaching, they come with a track record with many "first" milestones. Rachel Balkovec is no different. She fits the definition of a trailblazer:

- First woman to be a full-time manager for a Major League affiliated team (Tampa Tarpons 2022-2023).

- First woman to be a full-time hitting coach in an MLB organization (Yankees Florida Complex League team).
- First woman to serve as a full-time strength and conditioning coach in affiliated baseball (Tampa Tarpons).

All of these moves started, and kept signaling, a shift toward gender inclusivity in baseball, and now at the major league level. While there had been female coaches in MLB before, she was the first full-time hitting coach. The Yankees hire lends a high level of optimism about inclusion of females in MLB. I know that's been said before and now is said more often, but that truly is the case, and the more cases like this occur, the more it will be true.

The pathway for women to coaching has had its share of obstacles. Balkovec was denied low-level jobs in pro baseball because of her gender, even with the award of being the 2012 Appalachian League strength coach of the year (as an intern with the St. Louis Cardinals) on her resume. In addition to this, she spoke Spanish and had a master's degree in kinesiology to boot. Still denied.

All of this is a full reflection and impetus for Rachel and other women seeking similar paths into the world of baseball, at any level but especially at the major league level.

A former softball catcher at Creighton and the University of New Mexico, Rachel Balkovec got her first job in professional baseball as a minor league strength and conditioning coach with the Cardinals in 2012.

It is interesting to note that many of today's female major league coaches were catchers. It's a proven fact and talked about all around baseball that catchers make good managers and coaches. The position of catcher is unique because the catcher is the only player with the same perspective as the hitter. Eight players look toward the batter and home plate while the catcher stares back to align the defense. In addition, the catcher calls every pitch for the pitcher (fastball, curve etc).

On some days, the catcher's role can be the difference between winning and losing. It has been determined that catchers typically have high emotional intelligence, being able to manage their own game emotions while understanding the emotions of players around them. This contributes to a great intuitive feel for the game, an impressive characteristic of successful coaches and managers. Twelve of thirty MLB managers in 2019 were catchers in their playing days. The percentage in 2024 was slightly lower but still high. Rachel's catching background encompasses all of this.

Rachel's experience also includes baseball analytics, exercise science and kinesiology, and playing on an NCAA Division I softball team.

While working toward her master's degree at Vrije Universiteit in the Netherlands, she studied and researched human movement sciences, eye tracking for hitters, and hip movement for pitchers. All of this, backed by her passion, was in pursuit of a degree in biomechanics. This educational background offers Balkovec a very unique perspective for her overall coaching philosophy, strategies, and tactics, which in turn revolutionize her work in player development. Not a lot of major league coaches, male or female, have these credentials. It's no wonder she trailblazed as she did.

When the 2020 minor league season was canceled due to COVID, she went on to coach in the Australian Baseball League, followed by serving on the coaching staff for the 2021 SiriusXM All-Star Futures Game at Coors Field. All this, plus her experience with the Yankees, adds up (so far) to over ten years of working as a coach in professional baseball.

A common theme with MLB women and up-and-comers is that they are extremely driven. Luisa Gauci, an Australian born former co-worker with Rachel at Driveline, and a baseball player at the junior college level, said of Rachel's drive, "Being involved at these levels is where she wants to be. She's very headstrong. She was going to get there or anywhere she wanted to, no matter the circumstance." According to MLB writer Molly Burkhardt, Gauci has gone on to say that she is optimistic that in the near future, gender identity won't have to factor into hiring headlines: "I definitely see the next five years, like, that's not even going to be a question. There's going to be so many women being hired that there won't be enough reporters to report on it." There is a little bit of wishful thinking there but don't be surprised as to what really happens.

Balkovec understands that although she is considered a trailblazer, she says she has no problem stating that she is a product of the women who have come before her in sport. That is a common denominator of coaches interviewed for this book.

Alexia Jorge, who held a spot on the 2019 U.S. Women's National team development roster said along with Balkovec, "To really think that my dreams could come true through this, just because of other women trying to do what they're doing right now is amazing. It's insane. There is literally no other way to put it."

Upon Balkovec's hiring by the Yankees, she publicly stated, "Bias and stereotypes are going to be around forever, but I do think we've made a ton of progress. I mean, there's going to be more women in uniform next year. Looking back on those days it would have been incomprehensible to understand what the next decade was going to look like for myself and for others. And I do think we've made progress. Not in the numbers, but also just the way that people react to me and the way that they talk to me and it's becoming more normal. It's pretty apparent and it's just exciting to see how much progress we've made. We definitely have a lot of room to grow. But it's really exciting."

When Balkovec was named the Marlins' Director of Player Development, Commissioner Rob Manfred said, "I am pleased to see the game continue to make important progress at various levels. Major League Baseball is committed to providing a supportive environment for women and girls to pursue our sport as players, coaches, umpires, and executives. We are proud of Rachel, new Director of Player Development and all the women across our sport who are setting a positive example for our next generation of fans and proving, on and off the field, that baseball is a game for everyone."

Rachel's position gives her the spotlight to offer insight to others aspiring to such positions. The advice Balkovec would give is summed up as follows: "I tell people, the best thing you can do is just find the best person in the entire world in your field and go work for them for free. Just go and get the best information when you're first coming out of college, so you set yourself up with a solid foundation."

Her advice continues with her statement that if someone is going to do something extraordinary or work toward the top, there is no easy path. Excellence demands that a person do more and be better than everyone around them. Sometimes that means making sacrifices that nobody else has to make. She is adamant about this and finishes it by saying there are no exceptions.

In her quest to acquire expert knowledge, Balkovec relied on the advice of other female trailblazers. As a result, she is squarely focused on making sure other women follow in her footsteps. She said one way to change the hiring practices in professional baseball would be to increase the diversity of the candidate pools. "If you look at a coaching application process that you might get 300 resumes for, you might see one or two women who've applied for that job," she said.

In a story featured by the NCAA, Balkovec stated her hopes to see structural changes and new mindsets for women in sports. "We need to create more visibility, more pipelines to go, 'Hey, hey, hello, this is an opportunity for you. Females can and are doing what you are wishing for so go for it.'"

Balkovec wants to be a general manager, which Kim Ng was the first woman to accomplish when she took over front-office duties for the Marlins in 2020. The model is there for Balkovec to follow, but her nontraditional path to being manager in a professional dugout has her focused on the present.

There is no mistaking that on the field when coaching, Rachel cares very much for her players. She will say that she is a loving person but very direct when it comes to coaching. She has high expectations that come with great support and leadership, mostly by example. She knows the players are the ones to swing the bat and throw the ball. That's what she expects players to think about on the field. She doesn't feel that she has to coach them at every moment. She and all of her fellow coaches have that same expectations of players and coach when necessary.

As far as gender sensitivity, Balkovec has found that while the players may be curious about her at first, they appreciate and respect her work. She elaborated, "I do feel like they respect me. And at the very least they know that I'm passionate, hardworking, and I know what I'm talking about. Whether they like it or not is a different story. And every coach goes through that."

That leadership also comes in the form of being very honest with her players, after leading by example. She leads herself to show that she can lead others. Substitute the word "coaching" here for leadership; it takes on the same style. She also offers that anyone, players, coaches, and those that aspire, should not make excuses, should show up early, leave late, and put their heads down in difficult or challenging situations. That worked when she was playing and is working in her world of coaching.

Rachel did face gender discrimination early on. She will tell that in 2013, she was out of baseball because she could not get a major league interview of any kind. She was more than qualified and had to look for a way to overcome that bias. With the greatest of desires, she passed up paying non-baseball jobs to accept more internships, work her way through the network, and get what she wanted.

Rachel is not shy about stating her goal to become an MLB manager. She does, however, emphasize that she wants to do the proper learning before then. She offers this as advice to others along the way, be they young girls trying to get into the sport or those already involved and looking for advancement. She wants to excel at any job she is in and doesn't want to rush the process. She hopes that others will think that same way to make for a solid organization, wherever they are in the process.

Rachel Balkovec focuses on helping players improve, with a side focus of being visible in the sport. She believes that visibility is important to show others that jobs like hers are available, necessary, and becoming more commonplace.

Rachel is an advocate and continually talks about women coaches in the major leagues. She has gone so far to say (to MLB.com), "I don't think you sign your name on the dotted line to do something like this and then say, well, I don't want to be a role model. People ask why I am on social media...and it's like, I want to be a visible idea for young women. I want to be a visible idea for dads that have daughters. I want to be out there. And it's just I have two jobs and that's fine."

Finally, when asked about where she sees women in sports in the future, she states that because of how much change we have seen recently, things will be better and their presence almost common. Major League Baseball organizations are starting to ask for women's inclusion. Others are now asking her about other women to recommend for positions. She speaks of this as almost being in a dream world. Ten years ago, it was a dream, which is now becoming a reality.

Taylor Jackson—Turning a Lifelong Passion into A Career

Taylor Jackson is part of what is referred to as the first wave of female coaches in professional baseball. She truly has a lifelong passion, and it continues, as she finds ways of staying in the game and turning it into more than a labor of love. It is her career.

While Taylor does not consider herself a trailblazer or pioneer, she really is one by definition, as part of that first wave. At this writing Taylor is a performance coach with the Daytona (Florida) Tortugas, the single-A affiliate of the Cincinnati Reds. She describes that role as one with varied tasks, under the sports science umbrella of the franchise. With that, she works with the strength coaches in the sports science department, with some on-field responsibilities.

During games, Jackson will be in uniform. Sometimes she assists in the dugout, but often she'll reside in the bullpen with the relief pitchers.

Julio Morillo, the Tortugas field manager, says of Jackson, "She's very prepared, and very smart. Doing the homework, I know she's going to be doing, can help our pitchers know who they're going to be facing, how to start the at-bat, how to finish the at-bat, and I think it's a great asset for us."

Taylor Jackson has been involved in baseball in one way or another as far back as she can remember. She began her professional career in 2022 as a video coordinator for the Greenville (South Carolina) Drive, the Class A minor-league affiliate of the Boston Red Sox. Taylor Jackson entered the 2023 season as the team's first base coach, becoming the first female on-field coach in franchise history.

Being a female coach for an all-male team didn't seem like a novelty or anything out of the ordinary (though it was) to Taylor. She had always been around guys and baseball, so it was just a matter of course for her. She did say she grew up playing the game, as her dad played in college and passed the love of the game to her. Instead of playing softball like other girls, she played baseball on a mostly boys Little League team until she was fifteen. She did admit though, that it was cool if someone looked up to her and was inspired by her inclusion. To her, she just wanted to be around baseball, and still does.

When she didn't make the team at Tuscaloosa County High School, she still wanted to stay in athletics. Upon enrolling at the University of Alabama in 2016, she started working as a student assistant with the strength and conditioning staff for the Crimson Tide's different Olympic sports teams. This included the Alabama softball team, even though she really wanted baseball. She knew this would be one more step to that goal. She did find herself helping out with the Crimson Tide baseball team before graduating.

Jackson went to grad school at Louisiana Tech, working on a master's degree in Kinesiology-Sports Performance, and got an opportunity to help out on the field there. She then volunteered with Shelton State Community College as an assistant and stated, "I just found myself being drawn back to baseball a lot."

Her work at Louisiana Tech was a milestone in her career, as it was there that she realized that working in baseball is the path she wanted to pursue. One of her coaches at Tech said, "Taylor was just a pleasure to be around. Taylor is very intelligent, has a tremendous work ethic and an extreme desire to learn and grow. She literally just showed up and wanted to help with our program. It didn't take long for her to gain the respect of the coaches, players, and everyone within our organization. She has that hunger to succeed with zero ego. Anything she accomplishes in life will not surprise me."

While working on her master's degree, she was away from the sport. She knew she didn't want to end up in a lab somewhere and wasn't a fan of reading research papers one after another. Her desire was to be around and work with people and somehow make an impact through her work.

We offer these comments and quotes to share characteristics and traits that other females interested in baseball can follow.

Dr. David Szymanski, the Department Chair and Professor Director of Baseball Performance at Louisiana Tech, had this to say about Taylor Jackson, "I am proud of her for what she did while at Tech and what she has professionally accomplished. She is an example of how work ethic, desire, and selflessness can open doors for one's future."

Taylor's coaches had connections to the Boston Red Sox organization. In fact, one of her prior coaches, Bobby Sprowl, played for the team. Through networking with her baseball contacts and former coaches she was introduced to Sox scout Danny Watkins and was later hired as a video and technology intern. In that role, she ran the club's various high-speed tracking camera and software systems (such as TrackMan and Edgertronic) during games, batting practice, and bullpen sessions. She was involved in filming things from different angles, hitting and pitching, so the organization's analytics staff and coaches could look at the data generated and use it for player development.

The position of video intern is a common entry point to a Major League Baseball club. Other coaches have followed a similar path.

That job led Jackson to the Greenville Drive affiliate, a full-time coaching position where she did a little bit of everything and anything needed by the team and the other coaches. Her duties included coaching first base, helping out with the outfielders and baserunners in games, and with pre-game work. Working with and for the team's development coach, her job was to help out on the tech side of things and assist in bullpens and batting cages, as well as helping other coaches. Her work is what is known amongst the teams as the fourth coach. However, because fourth coaching roles are seasonal and often used as a rotation to bring in new talent, Taylor had to use her network again and pursue her next position elsewhere.

It's nice at this point in baseball history to hear that women are no longer considered all that unusual. With her baseball background and activity, she wasn't worried about any pushback from players due to the fact that she was female. She tips her hat to other female coaches who have come before her in recent seasons. This attitude is heard often from all other female coaches.

One of Taylor's coaching approaches is getting to know people, including other coaches, players, and the staff. As we have heard from other female coaches, showing them that you care is endearing and the right step in forming the proper relationships.

That is a common thread in her other work. A coach's caring nature consists of simply helping others get better. That's Taylor's coaching mentality. That sounds like common sense, but a proactive mentality like hers leads to success. Part of that mentality and action is to not only help players get better as a baseball player but many times as a person. Developing trusting relationships is key for a coach of any kind. Once trust is gained and the person being coached knows a coach is there to help them, the path to progress is easier.

In an interview with WVUA 23, a commercial television station owned and operated by the University of Alabama, she mentioned that she was always the only girl in baseball. She liked that. She viewed that situation as a challenge and thrived off it.

When asked about any gender-related challenges, she admitted nothing blatant came about. Taylor is at a point where female baseball coaching is much more common than it used to be. This helps eliminate discrimination and gender issues. She emphasizes that all of her teams have been very welcoming. Sure, there are always the locker room issues but even that is changing in today's times. She says she was always very respectful of the players' (and other coaches') space, and they respected hers, all while knowing that she was part of the team just like everyone else on the field.

Following up this discussion, Taylor was asked what advice she would give to young girls and other females aspiring to break into the game, specifically coaching. She started by saying her advice really applies to anyone, male or female. The biggest thing, she said, is to show that they care for people, show a genuine interest in them, and have the desire to help players get better. That's what coaching is all about. She furthers this by stating others should always ask where they can help. Much of the early work in coaching is volunteer work or internships with no or little pay. Not letting this get in the way is key. Anyone wanting to work in baseball has to have that foundational value of love for the game.

She concludes her words of advice with her suggestion to others to remember, "It's just a game. Sure, it's cool that we get to do this but put the time in, care for people and work hard."

Taylor never really saw her work and her roles as trying to break a barrier. It was just that she loved baseball and wanted to play. Her father knew this, as he often stated she wouldn't take the answer "no" when it came to anything related to the sport. She told him that someday she wanted to be part of MLB. Guess what? That happened. His message to her now is, "thanks for not saying no" along the way. He takes pride in the fact that many times she wanted to just go outside and have a catch, as Ray Kinsella said to his dad in the movie *Field of Dreams*.

There is no doubt, and she has even said publicly, that having confidence in what she knows and not getting discouraged is what keeps her going. Taylor is now coaching on her own field of dreams.

Perry Lee Barber—The Woman in Blue

It's 2024 and Jen Pawol is on the verge of becoming the first female umpire of a regular season MLB game after being given a full-time big league spring training schedule.

At the time of this writing, no woman has ever umpired a regular-season game. Pawol will be waiting for that call once the 2024 regular season begins.

Before Jen Pawol, there was and still is Perry Lee Barber.

Becoming a major league umpire is a long and challenging road. Just ask Perry Lee Barber. Typically, the journey starts in the minor leagues and can take years of hard work, many hours, miles of travel, dedication, and perseverance. Now add the female gender and it takes even harder work, greater dedication. and more perseverance. Perry Lee Barber has had such a journey.

Perry Barber has spent nearly fifty years umpiring in baseball, charting a course, and inspiring generations of girls and women. Her work as a professional baseball umpire has blazed a trail for female umpires and broken through barriers, increasing participation in a career previously reserved for the male gender. She is trying to level the playing field in baseball from an umpire's point of view.

She has worked in umpiring at all levels of baseball, both professional and amateur, including major league spring training and Division I college baseball, with international experience in the Caribbean, Taiwan, Japan, and many other countries.

From Jean Fruth's website, grassrootsbaseball.org:

> *Perry Barber has spent nearly a half-century umpiring in baseball, charting a course, and serving as the inspiration for generations of*

girls and women hoping to get involved in our National Pastime. The self-effacing lady umpire relishes her role as a beacon of hope. "We have a saying: 'If you can see it, you can be it.' How many girls would see women umpires out there and say to themselves, 'Wow. I didn't know women could do that!" Well, many have.

Perry's passion for baseball and her desire to be an active participant in the sport led her to pursue a career in umpiring at a time when such a choice was met with skepticism and resistance. In just her second game in 1981, Barber encountered a coach who took his Little League team off a baseball diamond in Palm Springs in protest of Barber's presence, as a woman, on the playing field. Undeterred, she persevered through the challenges, proving gender should never be a barrier to pursuing one's dreams in the world of sports.

This is straight from Perry Lee about her early interest in baseball: "I decided to educate myself and went to a bookstore one day and picked out a few books from the baseball section and started reading. I read *You Know Me Al* by Ring Lardner, *Eight Men Out* by Eliot Asinov, *Five Seasons* by Roger Angell, *A False Spring* by Pat Jordan, and *Pitching in a Pinch* by Christy Mathewson. By the time I stopped laughing over the hilarious Lardner stories, weeping over Asinov's finely crafted tale of the 1919 Black Sox, swooning over the poetry of Angell's prose, nodding in recognition of my own yearnings and failings in the pages of Pat Jordan's masterpiece, and marveling at the simple genius of one of baseball's best all-time hurlers-turned-scribe, I was hooked. The vast archive of baseball literature opened up a whole new world to me in which I immediately immersed myself."

It's always interesting to see how people get interested in the sport of baseball and the many paths that take them to the game.

Closecallsports.com reported that Barber credits historian Larry Gerlach's 1980 book *The Men in Blue: Conversations with Umpires* as steering her toward the umpiring craft, which has drawn assignments in high school, college, amateur, and international baseball, as well as assignor and supervisor responsibilities. She also has officiated several spring training exhibition contests and campaigned for women's inclusion in professional baseball.

Perry was asked when she realized she wanted to work in professional baseball. Her reply took her back to when she attended umpire school for the first time, in January of 1982. She went just to get trained and achieve some degree of proficiency, but once she was there, she got into the idea of making it into pro ball and following in the footsteps of Bernice Gera, Christine Wren, and Pam Postema, the only three women up to that point to have made it into pro ball umpiring.

Barber attended Harry Wendelstedt's umpire school in 1982-85 and 2005 along with her late twin sister, Warren, "so that we could always work together and guarantee that

I wasn't the only woman." She was assigned to several major league fantasy camps, most prominently the Mets' camp.

Barber's sister was her support system at the beginning when she received very little other support and appreciation. Barber has loads of stories about things said to her at games early in her career and things that happened because of her gender. She will tell you, though, that things are better now. There are more female umpires who are visible to players and fans. With this comes more of a willingness to accept the presence of a female in what has been typically a man's world. Perry Lee feels there aren't people standing in the way and gender inclusion is becoming more a way of life. She now calls it a sense of inertia. In this year's Wendelstadt umpiring class there are eight women. Perry Lee has been quoted as saying, "I won't rest until there are enough women out there once I leave the field for the last time to feel confident we're moving forward instead of stagnating, or worse, slipping backward toward a time when women really weren't welcome on the diamond."

Perry Lee's entre into professional baseball is one with many interesting twists and turns. In 2005 she went for an "audition" at the Mets fantasy camp that she was offered by Buddy Harrelson, the Mets' manager and the camp director. The front office people thought she did a decent job, and by the next year she was in charge of assigning umpires for all the major league fantasy camps (Mets, Phillies, Reds, Orioles, Red Sox).

Perry Lee shares the story of the day in 1985 when she was working a fantasy camp game that was part of the

Mets' spring training. During that time, the Mets' travel-ing secretary walked over and asked her if she would be interested in umpiring some intrasquad games. She admit-ted she wasn't sure what an intrasquad game was, but she jumped at the opportunity and three weeks later found herself umpiring a professional spring training game.

When asked about the reaction on the field when play-ers and coaches realize the umpire is a woman, Perry Lee offered that today it is no longer an anomaly. It hurt at first and along the way, but she is hearing it less and less as more women learn and participate in the sport.

Promoting diversity in baseball is top of mind for Perry Lee. Speaking for most advocates of female inclusion, she says we all want to see women playing, umpiring, manag-ing or being general managers: "My focus and the focus of most of the women is to open pathways at every level." It starts at the amateur level, to learn, feel welcomed and appreciated, have fun, and learn game and life skills. That in and of itself sounds like a mission statement. Maybe from there, females can move along the path to the major leagues. That of course, from Perry, includes female play-ers and female umpires.

Currently, Perry Lee conducts umpire clinics, speaks about umpiring and women's baseball, and serves as a board member for the International Women's Baseball Center and an advisor for Baseball for All.

As far as the future of women in baseball leadership positions, she views it as a "trickle up," proposition, where more participation will result in more growth. She says it won't happen in large numbers, but it will happen: an evolution of leaders, then followers who become new leaders. Others in addition to Perry Lee are making inroads and promoting a gradual change that is much needed, and according to her is long overdue.

Perry Lee's advice for young girls and females of any age for getting into baseball is simple and actually similar that of others already in the sport.

Firstly, it's almost common sense for anyone considering a career path to understand their passions. This extends to defining, identifying, and understanding values, passion, and purpose, all of which requires reflection and self-discovery. Each person must ask what truly matters to them.

Secondly, Perry Lee suggests finding a mentor with valuable knowledge to impart. She repeatedly emphasizes the importance of learning, learning, and learning some more. While this may seem like common sense, it's crucial. People seek successors who will continue the philosophies and practices of women in baseball today.

Thirdly, be prepared to make sacrifices and face pushback, which may come as female participation in baseball increases. Perry Lee stresses the importance of being willing to put in the work along the way. She observes that most female umpires do this out of love for the game and a desire to give back as they progress in their careers. Sometimes participating in lower-level games or with lesser-known teams can lead to opportunities for more prominent games and greater participation.

When speaking of Jen Pawol, potentially the first female to umpire a regular season major league game, Barber says, "When Pawol makes it to the bigs, I'll be thinking of my sister, who was my first steady partner, and of my mother, watching over her daughter as she umpired her first baseball game on a dusty, windswept, nondescript little diamond in the desert such a long time ago. The best thing is, it feels like I'm really only now getting started. So much is still possible." There is so much more to Jen Pawol's story and Perry Lee Barber's story. For now, we will credit their journey and cheer the progress and culmination of their trailblazing.

Perry Lee Barber is obviously a strong advocate for the next female major league baseball umpire, publicly stating she will not rest until a woman is on the major league staff. Things used to look bleak, but she said she is finally getting the feeling that the individual breakthroughs that are starting to happen are more than mere window dressing and checking gender boxes. She feels those changes signal a shift in the cultural attitude and acceptance, and the opening of opportunities at a faster rate. She says as one door opens, another glass ceiling shatters, and one more window opens just a little farther.

Perry's journey is not just about making calls on the field: it's a testament to resilience, determination, and the power to challenge norms. Perry Barber became a symbol of change, paving the way for more inclusivity in baseball. Her dedication and expertise as an umpire set a standard that inspired countless girls and women to follow their passion for the game, breaking free from the constraints of traditional gender roles.

As Perry Barber remains a presence in the world of baseball, her legacy serves as a reminder that diversity and inclusion enhance the richness of the sport. Her story is not only about calling strikes and balls; it's about breaking barriers, shattering stereotypes, and leaving a lasting impact on the future for aspiring female umpires and enthusiasts alike. Perry stands as a constant champion of women and girls who love and want to be part of the America's national pastime.

Rachel Folden—Right Where She Belongs

If someone in the world of baseball said winning is based on how many barrels you catch, would you understand? Would you know what that meant and how it could make a ballplayer successful? If not, let's let Rachel Folden help.

When researching baseball, you can find the Big Papi way of hitting or the Pete Rose way of baseball. There is even an Alex Rodriguez (ARod) way of hitting home runs. When asking Rachel Folden about her "way" of hitting she has a simple, concise, and complete answer: The Rachel Folden way of hitting is to catch as many barrels as possible. She further explains in this way that she doesn't care how a batter catches barrels, she doesn't care about their exact batting style, or even what coaching a batter listens to. It's often said a batter doesn't have to be perfect to hit. "Hitting with the barrel of a baseball up," refers to hitting a pitch hard with the sweet spot of the bat. This coincides exactly with the Rachel Folden way of hitting. Her goal, like that of many other coaches and hitting coordinators, is to eventually win games. According to Rachel, the way to win is to catch a lot of barrels.

Meet Rachel Folden, the Chicago Cubs' minor league hitting coordinator. When her hiring was announced, she became the first female coach in Cubs history. From then on she was, and is still, a prime figure for the evolution of women in professional baseball coaching and proof that women can have a place in a game long dominated by men.

Rachel explains her current role as one having a joint title. In addition to being the hitting coordinator for all the Cubs' minor league teams, she will serve as hitting coach for the Tennessee Smokies, their Double-A team that plays just outside Knoxville.

One of the media announcements said, "Rachel Folden spent much of her adult life smoking softballs over fences, so perhaps it's appropriate she'll be a coach with the Tennessee Smokies."

Folden said enthusiastically about this new part of her job, "Let's do this. It's a new challenge this year with a clubhouse full of a bunch of dudes and a leadership staff that is unmatched."

During spring training, that role is based at the Cubs camp in Mesa, Arizona. Late in spring training as players are sent down to the AA camp, Rachel will travel with them to start more focused coaching with that group.

Being amongst a bunch of male players is nothing new for Rachel. She grew up playing Little League baseball on an all-boys team, where she got used to being the only girl on the field.

These Little League days gave her a great desire for baseball. Although she excelled in her softball career, softball was not always her first choice. She does, though, say she had an incredible experience playing softball, increasing her passion and building her skills and knowledge while continually being intrigued more by baseball. She took this sense of intrigue and partnered with a baseball technology company working with the Cubs. That led to a strong recommendation by their key people to the team for her current position.

After a rigorous interview that included time with then-president of baseball operations Theo Epstein and general manager Jed Hoyer, she was hired.

While Rachel at first thought that her hire was to get a women into the Cubs coaching mix, she later found out and continues to prove the contrary. The Cubs quickly dismissed that thinking as well. Both Rachel and the team acknowledged early on that their working together had nothing to do with gender. The Cubs refuted that idea by saying, "Headlines are nice, but they don't win baseball games." Rachel feels the same way, discussing winning every chance she gets. She and the Cubs furthered that view by saying her work in revamping a hitting department is designed to provide the team with the best resources to win and succeed. Rachel Folden is a resource to do just that.

One funny story Rachel shares is that during her interview the question came up about what she would say or do if a bunch of players were standing around in their underwear after a game, having a beer and chatting. Rachel was quick to reply that she would say, "Can I have a beer too?" That answer obviously passed the interview test and she was well on her way.

Matt Dorey, who was senior director of player development when Rachel was hired and is now the vice president of player personnel, said at the time of her hiring, "We are always looking to get better. We felt like there was an opportunity to evaluate what was available and get back to our core values of providing the best in the industry experience for our players. We want to provide every tool we possibly can, to hold up our end to help our guys become part of the big leagues. Rachel has been working in the field of tech and data, leveraging all the newest technology." In her previous experience on and off the field she has incorporated biomechanics, science, data analytics, and technology into her sport and coaching. That went a long way with the Cubs. Dorey said, "We brought her in for an interview and she blew us all away. Her values lined up with the organization's core values."

In a report for milb.com, Rob Terranova quoted Dorey as saying after Rachel's start, "She's everything that we thought. She's hard-working, humble, and committed to the players. Her expertise and overarching passion for hitting beams through and she is a natural-born leader."

It's always interesting to watch the transitions of today's coaches into baseball and then coaching. Rachel played professional softball for the Chicago Bandits and Carolina Diamonds in the National Professional Fastpitch (NPF) league. During that time, she also jumped into coaching as a head coach for Encinal High School in Alameda, California and went on to be an assistant softball coach at Valparaiso University and Holy Names University.

Now as hitting coordinator, she is building her own staff of coaches and teaching players how to understand and use analytics and new technology, which is vital for today's professional baseball teams.

Folden says baseball and professional sports in general are seeing an influx of women with nontraditional backgrounds. The new breed of coach and in this case, a female coach, is good at digesting the data, applying technology, and communicating it at the right level to players. Folden says, "If a coach or hitting coordinator can communicate by speaking their language, at their level, that's coaching." That is consistent with Folden's passion to help players approach their top potential and succeed in the game.

Rachel Folden is a coach who in her pro softball days went through many of the things her players are going through. She has stated that her experience helps to, "level the playing field," in her communication and developing relationships with players.

Folden is not shy about stating that the players she works with have been welcoming and accepting of her from day one. Minor leaguers want to get better and get to the big leagues. If a coach is helping them do that, they will be accepted.

Pete Crow-Armstrong, an up-and-coming Cubs hitting star, worked with Rachel in the minor leagues. He stated of Rachel, "She's doing everything. She throws batting practice to us. She tries to strike us out. She mans the pitching machine. She is everywhere on the field and does everything really well. She's a smart, smart person."

When Rachel was hired, a former co-worker who was a biomechanical hitting consultant for the team said, "I think there is always going to be some pushback of bringing a female into what is considered a male sport, but Rachel transcends gender as she is so good at what she does. Gender doesn't matter." All those commenting said she can do well in an environment of mostly men.

In the milb.com story by Rob Terranova mentioned above, he reported Matt Dorey's comments related to breaking the gender barrier. Dorey stated, "We were just on the hunt for talent and the fact that she's a woman, it didn't even for a second prevent us from identifying her talent."

Cubs management said that because of Rachel's confidence and talent, she will cross the gender barrier just fine. Justin Stone, who was a hitting consultant for the Cubs, said to milb.com, "If somebody gives her crap, she'll get in the batting cage and probably outswing them."

Many of the women in female coaching roles get asked about gender challenges and handling anything related to a female being on an all-male team. Rachel Folden is no exception. She does say, however, that players do not care of she is female or not. She has a great knack of relating to them so the gender barrier, as she says, quickly came down. It took a little longer for staff to warm up to the whole gender-breaking concept. However, that mindset was soon quelled because of Cubs leadership's strong advocacy for females in coaching and specifically Rachel. She described it as almost having a "sponsor" on the job. She also said, "It took a minute for me to be judged just on my job."

Little things were present, like players who were afraid to curse or were extra cautious to not say something offensive to Rachel. But soon, and Rachel says very soon, players realized she was one of them and could be treated just like everyone else.

In talking with female coaches like Rachel, the subject of clothing always comes up. There is no line of baseball uniforms designed and made specifically for women. Rachel shared that Nike once tried to craft a female-designed uniform for female coaches and it fit fine, but she looked like a female in a female-designed uniform. She, and as it turns out, other female coaches, did not want to look different from their teammates on the field, which they did in the Nike uniform. As a result, she and other female coaches turned down Nike's gesture.

Rachel is an advocate, obviously, for women in professional baseball coaching. She uses social media to tell her of her successes and stories. She feels responsible for showing all women and others that gender doesn't matter. She was hired based on qualifications and that, together with her performance, will let her progress and keep her hired. She says she wants to show women in baseball and sports in general that someone can still do their job even amid talk of gender-related issues and challenges. She says, "Don't let it swallow you, just attack it and don't use it as a crutch."

Rachel says she feels that today, women don't necessarily shift their career path or jump into baseball coaching because they think they can't do it or they're not going to get a fair shot because of their gender. Her advice to those is, "Do your job really, really, well and be really qualified for it. When the time comes go after it and let your qualifications speak for yourself."

She does offer caution to MLB about just hiring females to coach. There are not necessarily a lot of women available with the right credentials, in part because they don't know that MLB coaching is a viable career. The key, as she suggests, is to hire qualifications. The more qualified females that are hired, the more visible they are to any and all others watching and learning.

It truly is a hope for Folden that she can inspire young girls who have a dream of working in major league ball. She wants young girls to know that there is room in the game for them. She hopes her visibility will bring more interested women into the game and coaching.

Rachel appreciates the role Justine Siegal played when she entered the league as the first woman to throw batting practice to a major league team. She feels Justine and others have helped things progress to a point where a woman on the baseball field is, as she says, normalized.

One last comment she offered on diversity is that it is her goal and probably the goal of other female coaches is to become diverse amongst themselves. Right now, female coaches are lumped in as a group of "female coaches." They truly are all different, have unique qualifications, and want to be known for that, not as being part of a group of female coaches.

Rachel is proud of her work, her players, and her organization. She says, "It's a good time to be a hitter in the Cubs organization." Rachel is not sure of her future. However, she loves coaching the players with their hitting and loves the whole concept of player development. For now Rachel Folden is where she belongs, in batting practice, firing changeups, breaking balls, and fastballs and helping players catch as many barrels as possible.

Gretchen Aucoin—When Preparation Meets Opportunity

The Roman philosopher Seneca first uttered those famous words, "Luck is what happens when preparation meets opportunity." That saying is often quoted by hard-working dreamers everywhere. Gretchen Aucoin is one of them. The opportunities placed in front of her continue to lead to a series of fortunate events. Is that luck? Refer to Seneca.

There is a lot to Gretchen's college softball career: joining one team on scholarship, wanting more, and transferring to another. She clearly had an objective of being a leader and leaving a college legacy she could be proud of.

She continued to lead by example and often told others to keep working toward their dreams (like her) and they would find that anything is possible. With her upbringing in the small Gulf Coast town of Ocean Springs, Mississippi, she said if a small-town girl like her can make it, get opportunities, and succeed, then there is a chance that anyone can. Again, refer to Seneca.

After her successful college career and with her future still a bit unclear, a former college teammate approached her and asked if she was interested in playing professional softball for a team in New Zealand. She was at a point where she literally thought, "Why not? That is a question often asked of those presented with opportunity.

The initial opportunity to play in New Zealand came unexpectedly, but Gretchen's willingness to seize the chance demonstrated her readiness for such opportunities. The subsequent invitation to join the Cleveland Comets in the National Professional Fast Pitch League further exemplifies how her preparation in college and dedication to the sport created opportunities. Again, she was faced with an opportunity and decided to go for it. That lasted a couple of months, then it was off to New Zealand.

Fast forward: Gretchen ended up being the league's most valuable player.

According to *Baseball Jobs Overseas*, a coach she had for two seasons said, "She was a major part of our success that season." Craig Montvidas, an American, added, "She's very, very disciplined and one of the most professional players I've coached, and I've coached more than twenty

Olympic athletes, pros in the U.S., and national team players. You'd give her something to do, and you knew it would get done. Coaching would be very simple if all players were like her." *Baseball Jobs Overseas* provides a dependable, specialized service for aspiring and established professional baseball and softball players and coaches looking to take their career overseas.

During a following summer she played for the Bussolengo softball club based in Verona, Italy and helped to lead that team to the Italian Championship.

Playing for the Bussolengo club was another opportunity for Gretchen Aucoin.

Opportunity? How about another one? Gretchen's older brother was playing baseball in Germany while on a mission trip. After joking that it would be good if she could play on that team, it happened. It was her first time trading softball skills for hardball skills. Even the unplanned transition to baseball in Germany, inspired by a casual joke, turned out to be a crucial moment for Gretchen. Gretchen states the opportunity to play baseball opened up her eyes to the fact that girls could play and be involved in the game. Little did she realize it was a steppingstone for things to come with the NY Mets.

Did it just happen? Was it luck? Call it being at the right place at the right time but again, refer back to Seneca. Her preparation and experience had met opportunity and it looked like luck, but it just happened.

One of Gretchen's former teammates and coaches in New Zealand stated, "She's always striving to be the best but also knows when to take a step back mentally and analyze situations. She understands what she needs to do to succeed." This quote highlights her dedication to excellence and her ability to analyze situations strategically. This mindset, competitiveness, and desire to succeed, combined with her hard work, created a foundation for success.

After a Covid-canceled softball season, Gretchen landed with a nearby New Zealand team in Wellington, the capital of New Zealand, as the Lower North Island softball development officer. Again, another opportunity was right at her doorstep. One door closed with Covid, and another one opened. Little did she know at the time that her development officer job would prepare her for what would be next with the NY Mets.

Having just a bit of baseball experience, she thought she would return to the U.S. and pursue something related to softball. She wasn't sure of her path upon her return, but lo and behold, opportunity rose again for Gretchen. After meeting and networking with Rachel Balkovec, now the director of player development for the Miami Marlins, she was referred to the management of player development for the Mets, was interviewed, and landed the position as a player development coach for the club's minor league team system.

While Gretchen's path may seem rapid and spontaneous, it is evident that her success is rooted in continuous preparation and a willingness to embrace opportunities as they arise. It aligns with the idea that at first glance, her achievements may appear to be luck, but upon closer examination, they are the result of a combination of preparation and the ability to recognize and capitalize on her chances. It all wasn't planned as a straight path. She just worked hard, was presented with opportunity, and jumped. Gretchen has said, "I seem to always be hungry for more. I wanted more professionally as I knew there was more out there to grab."

Opportunities rose quickly. She looked to others like an overnight success but that "overnight" really was two to three years in the making. Yes, it was quick but she built the foundation along the way.

"Coaching and development kept calling me," Gretchen said. "I had experience as a development officer with a job to help the sport, baseball and softball, grow in the New Zealand community that I was in for men and women." This was part of what the Mets noticed.

Another opportunity was present when the Mets came calling and hired Gretchen as a coach in their minor league player development team. She was one of the few women with on-field coaching positions in affiliated baseball and the first ever in the Mets organization.

The Mets saw in Gretchen a strong work ethic, a great demeanor with teammates, players and coaches, competitiveness, and a real understanding of the work environment in high-level sports.

"Player development was in my wheelhouse of skills. I had a passion for it and was building experience with it," she said. "The Mets liked my ways of going about teaching, instructing, and presenting in my coaching. I still approach things with a learning attitude to always try to better what I am doing. I'm learning new things, new methods, new ways to coach players and I love it." She continued, "Right now, I am right in the middle of getting to know staff and players and what really is needed from a developmental point of view. I'm hugging each discipline finding where I can grow and what players need what along the way."

None of this was planned, nor did she plan on becoming a trailblazer for women, whether playing or coaching. She talks about the fact that she has always landed on a platform of leadership and pushing her limits. She was always cognizant of setting an example, again whether playing or coaching. Now it has hit her that her scale of setting an example is at a whole new level.

The more you observe Gretchen, the more it is evident that it is her demeanor, attitude, and personality that line her up for opportunities.

Gretchen realizes there is a gender gap. She offers a perspective on communication, emphasizing the importance of understanding others, building trust through relationships, and maintaining confidence in her approach, especially when trying to convey information in a way that connects with different individuals. It's clear that she values the human aspect of interactions and believes in the power of building connections to overcome potential barriers. She sums that up by saying we are all just humans, not men and women.

As far as the attention that comes with trailblazing and her new platform, she doesn't like it, but she says she can handle it. She emphasizes that she doesn't "soak" in it. Gretchen says, "Doing what I am doing is new to others but not me. It's based on my experience and foundation that has led me to this point."

Gretchen offers a point of reflection, "If I had to reflect on some things that I've learned along the way up to this point I would say to take opportunities that keep coming. It's OK to say 'Why not?' I didn't always realize where those opportunities would lead me to, but I took them. I know and always knew that if I work hard these opportunities will lead to something good and then I will decide on the next step. Lots of changes in a quick period of time allow me to live freely and not pressure myself about what's next or my path."

She goes on to say, "I am enthusiastic about leveraging social media and other platforms to provide visibility for opportunities, particularly for the next generation. My advice to the upcoming generation about hard work, seizing opportunities, and having the courage to pursue their goals is valuable and empowering. Encouraging them to consistently put in effort and take advantage of the opportunities that arise will certainly contribute to personal and professional growth."

Yes, she knows she is breaking barriers and inspiring the next generation. She likes that she is creating a role model for others that she would have liked to have had when she was younger. She is now one of those trailblazers, what she would have called the "front women" paving the way for the next generation, and that generation is not far behind. She respects the others that came before her. She calls them graceful with a strong demeanor. The bottom line is she wants to show others they can do something similar a lot sooner than she did or sooner than they think.

Gretchen Aucoin's journey is a testament to the synergy between preparation and opportunity. Seneca's insight captures the essence of how individuals like Gretchen can turn seemingly fortuitous events into successful outcomes through their hard work and readiness to embrace chances. It's really all the result of a proactive and well-prepared approach to life's possibilities. Gretchen's story exemplifies the power of being ready for opportunities and the role this mentality plays in creating one's success.

Amanda Kamekona—Serious About Baseball

Stepping into Amanda Kamekona's home, you'll encounter a charming presence named Mickey Mantle. No, not the legendary baseball player himself, nor his ghost. In this household, Mickey Mantle is a lively 1½ year old Maltese, lovingly described by Amanda as a fighter, survivor, rescue dog, and 2.4 pounds of pure personality!

Naming dogs after famous figures, be they celebrities or sports icons, is a common practice. It not only offers a wide array of options but also helps to reflect a dog's demeanor and, at times, the owner's own persona. Moreover, it allows owners to pay homage to their favorite personalities or interests.

For Amanda, naming her beloved pet after a legend like Mickey Mantle underscores her profound passion for the sport. Every time she calls her dog, it serves as a joyful reminder of the excitement and fulfillment baseball has brought into her life. Amanda Kamekona, known mostly as AK, is serious about baseball.

AK's seriousness has propelled her to her current position. Major League Baseball's Cleveland Guardians made history in 2023 by hiring her as the first woman field coach in team history. As the hitting development coach, she will be based at the team's complex in Goodyear, Arizona where she will focus mainly on rookie league players. Her position as the first woman hired by the Guardians for an on-field role continues the MLB trend of bringing more women into the game.

When talking with AK about all of this, you can hear glee and total excitement in her voice, her dialogue, her descriptions, and when talking about her passion (baseball and not her dog, in this case).

Amanda was actively involved in baseball up until her junior year in high school, including playing travel baseball. Despite her passion for the sport, she acknowledged that her 5'2" stature limited her abilities, which prompted her move to softball. With her parents unable to afford college tuition, they encouraged her to pursue a scholarship, leading her to excel in fast-pitch softball and ultimately earn a scholarship to UCLA.

Her journey in softball was rich with experience, from playing to coaching and even founding her own travel team. A pivotal moment came when Rachel Folden, coach and coordinator for the Chicago Cubs and a friend and former teammate of Amanda's, texted her about a potential MLB opportunity, "Cleveland's looking for a hitting coach and I think that you'd be a really good fit." Despite initial uncertainty due to the scarcity of female coaches in Major League Baseball, Rachel assured her the Guardians were seeking a hitting coach and gender was not a barrier.

Amanda interviewed with both the Guardians and the Cubs, primarily due to Folden's recommendation, but ultimately chose to join the Guardians. She went through a long interview process that determined she was the best candidate for the job. Her hiring marked a significant step forward, highlighting the evolving landscape of gender inclusivity in major league coaching.

After a year at Cleveland's developmental complex, she moved to an assistant hitting coach position with Cleveland's AA affiliate, the Akron Rubber Ducks. Looking at the team's online roster of coaches, you will find six coaches, with her the only female.

AK is described by the general management group of the Guardians as a dynamic coach, excited about learning and helping players develop. Excitement about her hiring pervades the organization. At the time, Guardians assistant manager James Harris stated, "We were hiring a hitting coach, we weren't hiring a female hitting coach. She's qualified and she's experienced." That's exactly the point where some areas of baseball have progressed, not singling out gender-specific coaches. Not all baseball has advanced to that point.

One interesting item reported by Mandy Bell, Guardians beat reporter for MLB.com, is that out of everything AK has done to decorate her resume, coaching with an under age ten (U-10), travel ball team was one of her favorites. That was a great teaching experience. According to the MLB.com report, Kamekona stated, "When an athlete is struggling to understand something you're saying, it's to go OK, 'If I had to explain this to a ten-year-old, how would I do that?' Typically, that helps us get on the same page to then foster more in-depth conversation, coaching and teaching after." That's what that U-10 coaching experience offered. Never would she have expected to use these tactics with professional baseball players but now she does.

AK also points out that many baseball skills and tactics are trickling into softball and vice versa. She states plainly that an elite swing is an elite swing in either sport.

One key to her job is developing relationships with the younger hitters in the organization and focusing on improving hitting on the field as well as the coaching tactics to do so.

An MLB.com reporter said, "Kamekona almost has to pinch herself at times to remind herself where she is. The little girl who effortlessly picked up the game of baseball at a middle school tryout is suddenly in a professional baseball uniform, walking across the field of a spring training game, ready to observe her coworkers and coach." Kamekona replies to this by saying that she is really lucky to call what she is doing "work."

When questioned about players' initial reactions to a female coach, she remarked that gender-related comments are virtually non-existent. In her experience, athletes are singularly focused on improvement. At her current level, all players share the goal of reaching the major leagues. As long as a coach demonstrates the ability to help them achieve that goal, players, in her words, "don't care if you are an alien, purple, man, or woman." Their priority is to do whatever it takes to get to the show (the major leagues), and advance to the highest level of competition, irrespective of factors such as gender, race, or color.

Regarding coaching, AK states, "I haven't encountered any situations where I feel that gender has hindered or been an issue. However, there was one incident that stands out as a significant compliment from a male coworker. I asked this coworker, another hitting coach, who is male, for his opinion on perfumes, wanting to know which one he liked best. He was surprised and remarked that he had completely forgotten that I was female until moments like these. He said he only knew me as AK, the assistant hitting coach working alongside him, not AK, the female assistant hitting coach. This compliment resonated with me, highlighting a sense of gender transparency in our relationship. I consider my rapport with all coworkers to be 'phenomenal,' and the same as this regarding gender."

The same situation exists with athletes. Across the board, women are new in baseball, so locker rooms and clothes are different, but her Cleveland Guardians club is very supportive of gender transparency. All player-coach relationships are gender transparent.

AK was asked about her own individual efforts to proactively promote diversity within the ranks of Major League Baseball. Personally, she is not someone who likes a lot of attention.

She does, however, make it a point to be very visual and active on social media, showing what she is doing in her job and role. Her effort is to let women and girls know that women are doing what is traditionally a male job and being successful. Within all of this she includes discussion about her female counterparts in baseball. When women get to the major leagues, she wants them to know there is a support group of other women to lean on for mentoring and experience. Also you can bet there is a picture or two of Mickey Mantle the dog on her social media posts.

AK mentioned that the Cleveland Guardians organization has its own diversity and inclusion program and effort that they deliver, with a whole dedicated department. On their website you will find the following message:

> The Cleveland Guardians are committed to developing and maintaining an environment that embraces all forms of diversity to enrich our core values, enhance our competitive position, strengthen our impact within our community, and foster a greater sense of belonging for our employees.

Inherent in our role as a civic institution, we strive to unite and inspire our city with the power of team. We have a long, yet imperfect history of doing this as an organization, but we are committed to making a difference. We know that sports can be a powerful agent of change in our society, and it is our hope that we can use our platform to be a part of the positive change we need in our country.

At the Cleveland Guardians, we commit our-selves to building a community that values and celebrates differences, encourages dia-logue, fosters mutual respect, and highlights our shared purpose and beliefs. In pursuing our purpose to unite and inspire our city with the power of team, we embrace diversity, equity, and inclusion as strategic and moral imperatives in our work. We define diversity, equity, and inclusion to ensure common un-derstanding across our community players, staff, and fans. (Source: mlb.com/guardians.)

AK advises women interested in coaching to con-nect with accessible coaches, like herself. She emphasizes the transparency and honesty within their community, encouraging aspiring coaches to ask questions about coaching as a female and how to break into major league coaching. AK stresses the importance of pursuing one's passion and interests, despite potential challenges and becoming part of the female coaching community.

She also offers a word of caution, noting that the path may not always be easy. She says, "It's not all sunshine and rainbows. There will be roadblocks or detours. There will be questions of why you are doing this and why do you want to pursue something in a male dominated world. Know in those moments there will be a lesson or preparation for future career developments. While these hurdles may seem insurmountable at times, they can ultimately provide valuable experiences and insights that will prove beneficial in the long run."

At this point, it's clear that AK is just getting started. She is settling into her new role as assistant hitting coach for the Cleveland Guardians and developing relationships with the younger and newer hitters in the organization. Ultimately, her focus is on enhancing the hitting performance of the team. Watch for her and Mickey Mantle on your screen of choice.

Ronnie Gajownik—Making Her Path and Trailblazing

During the 2024 NBA All-Star weekend, Steph Curry and Sabrina Ionescu competed in the first three-point challenge between the NBA and the WNBA. This historic matchup, seen by many as transcending gender boundaries, pitted two of basketball's finest shooters against each other for the first time. Despite Ionescu's formidable skills, Curry emerged victorious, solidifying his status as one of the best three-point shooters in basketball history.

Following the competition, Ionescu emphasized the importance of skill and determination over gender with the heart and being the best qualifier, stating, "Tonight shows a lot of young girls and young boys that, if you can shoot, you shoot. It doesn't matter if you are a girl or a boy. I think it matters the heart that you have and wanting to be the best that you can be."

Ronnie Gajownik shares this same mindset and philosophy, believing in the value of skill, determination, and the drive to be the best, regardless of gender.

Ronnie Gajownik is making history and trailblazing as a female in the male-dominated world of Major League Baseball. In 2023, she became the field manager for the Arizona Diamondbacks' minor league Hillsboro Hops in Oregon, making her the first woman to manage at the high-A level. In 2024 she was promoted to bench coach of the Diamondbacks' AA affiliate, the Amarillo Sod Poodles.

Gajownik agrees with Sabrina Ionescu that it doesn't matter if you are a girl or a boy in competition. She rounds that out with a similar sentiment by saying, "We all have ten fingers and ten toes. It all boils down to passion and doing the right thing when you are the right person." The same holds true, according to Gajownik, when coaching on the baseball field.

It was evident throughout the NBA's three-point competition that the spirit of camaraderie and mutual respect prevailed, emphasizing the unity and inclusivity within the basketball community, and celebrating the diversity of talent within the sport. The event represented a step forward in promoting gender equality in sports by demonstrating that skill and ability transcend gender boundaries, and highlighting the importance of recognizing and celebrating talent regardless of gender.

While this book is not about basketball, it is about similar intentions and reality in the sport of baseball. In baseball, as in basketball, that mindset can truly make a difference. Ronnie Gajownik represents this spirit loud and clear and is charging forward.

As bench coach of the Sod Poodles, she is second in command of the team. After a year of being first in command of the Diamondbacks' high-A level team, she is in another position to learn and show her coaching and management skills.

According to the MLB glossary, a bench coach is considered the right-hand man (or in this case the right-hand woman) to his (her) team's manager. Bench coaches assist their managers in decision-making and sometimes relay scouting information from the front office to the players.

The bench coach typically steps in to act as manager when the regular manager is unavailable (often as a result of being ejected from the game). Many bench coaches eventually become managers themselves.

Gajownik further states that her job, as in past coaching, is to develop relationships with players, to help the manager with specific players and skills, to coach at first base, and fully support the manager, his strategies, and tactics. In short, she does anything and everything that the manager needs for team support. Gajownik once described her bench coach's role as Robin to the manager's Batman.

Gajownik began her tenure in the Diamondbacks organization as a video assistant for the High A Hillsboro Hops, a role that has led many future coaches into the pipeline. Following that she coached in the Arizona Complex League and moved to her current team, the Amarillo Sod Poodles, halfway through the season. For the rest of that season she served as a first base coach, worked with outfielders, and performed other coaching duties.

Gajownik's interest in the national pastime began early. As the only child of avid Chicago Cubs fans, she often found herself having a catch with her dad. He took her to many MLB spring training sessions as a young child. Her playing career began with T-ball and then softball, the natural path for girls at the time. After softball, she was introduced to Team USA women's baseball, where her play led to a gold medal in the 2015 Pan-American Games, the first to feature women's baseball as a medal event.

During and right after the Covid pandemic, Ronnie participated in organized remote networking events which led to an introduction to Kim Ng.

Ng, a baseball pioneer and former general manager of the Miami Marlins, noticed Gajownik and asked her about her interest in Major League Baseball. Gajownik did the routine duty of sending out resumes, after expressing her interest and desire to Ng, and participated in the MLB-sponsored Take the Field program.

From MLB:

MLB hosts the Take the Field program, a two-day event at the annual Winter Meetings specifically designed for women interested in front office and on-field careers within professional baseball. Take the Field provides opportunities for education and engagement with Club and League personnel through panels, breakout sessions and professional development.

The event offers women an opportunity to learn from current baseball employees, develop in their areas of interest and network with their peers and other baseball professionals. Sessions focus on analytics, baseball operations, coaching, player development, replay, scouting and umpiring, as well as leadership, communication, and technology in baseball.

At the event and afterward, Gajownik ended up talking with and interviewing with three MLB teams. She set her sights on the Diamondbacks, saying she, "liked the vibe." She had good conversations with their manager of baseball technology and other management leaders of the Diamondbacks, which resulted in her offer of the role of video assistant.

I asked Ronnie what gender issues she has run into whether playing, coaching, interviewing, or in her current role, and she was almost at a loss to come up with anything significant. Most of what is considered a challenge is more media-generated.

It's encouraging that the question of gender is somewhat less significant than it used to be, but by nature of this book it is still in the public spotlight.

Gajownik further commented that when asked about gender-related issues with players, she says, whether it's a cliché or not, "Players don't care what you know until they know that you care for them." She states that you have to earn the right to be in a position like hers and that players and other coaches recognize that fact.

She did relay one instance of what could be called non-inclusion because of her gender. In a Hillsboro Hops game, with her as the manager, a play on the field required an umpire's judgement. In these situations, the umpire normally goes to the manager to explain the ruling. Gajownik was in the third base coaching box at the time and the umpire went straight to the dugout looking for a manager. Though minor league managers usually serve as third base coaches during games, this umpire didn't allow himself to think this female coach was the manager he needed to talk to. He explained his ruling to the men in the dugout, which actually is a rules violation. That was his mistake. The umpire later apologized to Ronnie, saying he had never encountered a female manager. That, according to Ronnie, was the only on-field blunder she experienced. It seemed minor but it happened because of gender.

Ronnie experienced no gender issues in any of her job interviews. As she puts it, she has ten fingers and ten toes and the team was focused on hiring the right person for the job, so gender didn't matter. This is a significant sign of the progress of inclusion in MLB.

From all of this, her experience to date and her feeling of inclusion, she does have a message to young girls and other females wanting to pursue a career in Major League Baseball. She adamantly states, "Even if you don't see a path to where you want to be you can make one. If you do the right things if you're the right person, figure out what you need to do to get to that spot." She recounted Sabrina Ionescu's statement when competing against Steph Curry, "It doesn't matter if you're a boy or a girl if you can shoot you can shoot."

Her advice continues, "Just because you don't see a woman in the sport doesn't mean you can't be there. There are more women coming into the sport. If you're passionate about something, go out and do it." She makes a point to say that her game appearances are showing young girls that they too, can grow up and coach in baseball. She often says, "If you can see it you can believe it," much like others who say and have been quoted, "If you can see it you can be it."

Gajownik states that players, generally, do not bring up gender anymore. She is building relationships and has earned her position, and players know that.

Early in her Diamondbacks career, Ronnie had the opportunity to spend time with the current Diamondbacks manager, Torey Lovullo. They actually sat side by side during a pre-season split squad game as a training opportunity for Gajownik. Lovullo publicly stated his support of Ronnie's path in Major League Baseball and the Diamondbacks. As reported by Steve Gilbert, a reporter for MLB.com covering the Diamondbacks, Lovullo said, "I've just appreciated my time with her. I think she's a spectacular teacher and can relate to the players very well." Lovullo added, "I've been in baseball a long time, and unfortunately, it's taken the game this long to get this far, but it's moving very quickly in the right direction and I'm happy about it. There have been a lot of pioneers out there, and to all those women that have taken chances that have given Ronnie this opportunity, I commend them."

All in all, Ronnie Gajownik is very happy with her decisions and path into Major League Baseball. Her values and principles come out loud and clear as she talks. She mentioned repeatedly and closed our conversation with:

- "I see more and more, men in Major League Baseball and all around the sport are advocates for females in the sport and females coaching teams."
- "I'm in the relationship-building business. The right to be in positions like ours has to be earned. The position goes to the right person regardless of gender. That's the way it should be."
- "I focus on doing my job right, my job as a friend, coach, mentor, teammate, wife, family and more."

As far as the future is concerned, Ronnie shared words of wisdom from her mother, "Be happy and be where your feet are. The opportunities will come." With her path, her experience, her drive, and her passion, those opportunities are hers for the taking and she is happy where her feet are.

Sara Goodrum—Progressing as Part of Baseball's Business

The Miami Marlins made a notable addition to their baseball operations department when they hired former Houston Astros Director of Player Development Sara Goodrum as Director of Special Projects.

Goodrum, fresh off overseeing the Astros' minor league system for the past two seasons, brings a wealth of experience to the Marlins. Prior to that, she worked in the Milwaukee Brewers organization, serving as their minor league hitting coordinator in 2021.

While the exact details of her role remain undisclosed, the "Director of Special Projects" title hints at her involvement in key initiatives. This could involve player development, where she could use her expertise to enhance the Marlins' minor league system or identify new talent. Additionally, her understanding of analytics and scouting might contribute to integrating these areas into the team's decision-making process. Furthermore, Goodrum's arrival marks a positive step toward increasing diversity within the Marlins' front office, potentially leading to inclusivity efforts at more levels.

The move signifies the Marlins' commitment to innovation and fresh thinking. Goodrum's distinct set of skills and experience are expected to bring a new perspective to the organization, potentially leading to changes in player development, scouting, and overall strategy.

Sara Goodrum is another pioneer in the world of female coaching in Major League Baseball. As is becoming the norm, and much like all players and coaches, movement is from team to team and promotion to promotion. That's all as part of the business of baseball and the management of baseball organizations.

Goodrum played softball for the University of Oregon from 2012-15, when the Ducks appeared in the Women's College World Series three times. Sara graduated with a degree in human physiology, followed by a master's degree in exercise and sports science from the University of Utah.

After an internship and a role as coordinator of integrative sports performance for the Brewers, she became the Brewers minor league hitting coordinator, making her the first woman in baseball history to serve in that role. (Her official title was Coordinator—Hitting Development Initiatives.)

Goodrum oversaw the hitting program and curriculum for all of the Brewers' minor league players and hitting coaches, while traveling to all of the team's affiliates to assist in player instruction.

Sara said at the time of her assignment, "Let's start making our hitters become the best they can possibly be. I get to talk about what I love—and that's hitting."

For any woman moving within an organization or between organizations, in baseball or any other field, there is always a concern of how they will be received, especially for a woman entering a job or field dominated by the male gender. In Sara's experience, the hitters she has instructed and coached have shown no bias. She went on to say, "The most eye-opening thing for me—especially with the players coming up now—they don't care if you're a man or a woman. If you can provide them with information and guidance that's going to help them accomplish making it to the big leagues, they don't care." This is a common attitude among women players.

Sara states, "For me, it's always about showing first and foremost that I care about the players. I'm going to continue to do that as I go into the role of being a little more on the front line with our players. Showing them, 'I want to help you guys in your career, and I'll be able to provide that information.' Our hitting coaches are phenomenal, as well. I don't think the players mind what your gender is. It's about the information and care."

Many of the women coaches interviewed repeatedly said players at the lower levels only think about one thing, and that is what can they do, how can they improve to get to the big leagues. That was the case with Sara's players.

Like many players, coaches, and particularly female coaches Sara thanked and gave credit to her parents as being her biggest role models. They pushed, helped, and encouraged her to pursue her dreams of working in sports and being a major league coach. The staff of the Brewers also encouraged her. She has been quoted as saying that with all of this encouragement and the players' reaction, she knew this is what she wanted to do. Sara said, "Coaching and a role like this has always been at the forefront of my mind. I feel at home when I'm on a baseball field. It brings so much joy to me."

David Stearns, the Brewers' general manager at the time of her tenure, said, "I think we've seen that because of her talent and her skill set, she is trusted and respected."

General managers and fellow coaches' perceptions, thoughts, and opinions are very important to promotions like Sara's. Starting out and continuing on the right foot usually can result in success, which Sara has had.

Said Tom Flanagan, who was the Brewers' farm director at the time of Sara's promotion, "I think gender is really a non-issue, where we're at today in the game. Specifically, with Sara, there is a familiarity with our hitters. She has been around the batting cage for the last couple of years, so there are relationships there, there's knowledge of what we're trying to do and what she's trying to do."

Also at the time, Brewers director of player development initiatives Jake McKinley said, "She is an elite technician of hitting, has great feel for people and is an awesome human being." That endorsement is a recipe for success, male or female.

Sara then took a position as director of player development with the Houston Astros, making her one of the most visible and highest-ranking female executives in baseball at the time. That job lasted almost two years (or two seasons), until newly hired general manager Dana Brown wanted to reshape his front office, put his own stamp on the organization, and move in a different direction, according to him.

Fast forward to February 2024 when the Miami Marlins announced what they considered as a notable addition to their baseball operations department by hiring Goodrum as director of special projects.

While the exact details of her role were not made public, it was assumed that by virtue of her title that she would be involved in various key initiatives. This suggested the role could involve player development, where her expertise and experience could enhance the Marlins' minor league system or go as far as identifying new talent in and outside the organization. Additionally, it was reported that her understanding of analytics and scouting might contribute to integrating these areas into the team's decision-making, development, and coaching processes. It was said at the time that Goodrum's arrival marks a positive step toward increasing diversity within the Miami Marlins' front office after the era of Kim Ng, potentially leading to more inclusivity efforts at all levels.

Any time an organization makes a move like this and reports it like this, it signifies they have a commitment to innovation, fresh thinking, and inclusion. Goodrum's diverse skillset and background are expected to bring what the Marlins consider a new voice to the organization, potentially leading to more positive changes.

Goodrum is a pioneer. She broke barriers, blazed trails, and is continuing her climb. She obviously has been part of the business of baseball where leadership changes alter the underlying organization and ignore gender as a qualification. In the case of the departure from the Astros that was classified as moving in a new direction, that was probably true and not media code or PR spin for anything other than a new GM putting his own touch on an organization. In this case Sara was not consistent with Dana Brown's philosophy, but has landed on her feet. At the time of this writing there was not much more to report about her new position other than what is written here. Regardless, it marks another female being part of a Major League Baseball organization and a continuance of blazing the path of females in baseball.

VI. Profiles of Success

Leading Women in MLB Front Offices

===

This book highlights both coaches and front office women in baseball. It's important to look at the remarkable journeys, personal and professional, that led them to these heights.

Today more C-suite positions than ever are filled by women, and the number is growing. In a review of all thirty MLB front office rosters, these are just some of the many titles women hold:

- Chief Financial Officer
- Chief Marketing Officer
- Chief Communications Officer
- Chief Legal Officer
- Chief Public Affairs and Communications Officer
- President of Business Operations
- Chief Diversity Officer

- Chief Development Officer
- Chief Experience Officer
- Chief Revenue Officer

In an August 2023 article for *Sports Business Journal*, Erik Bacharach reported that Marti Wronski, the Milwaukee Brewers' longtime general counsel, was promoted to chief operating officer. At that time, she was the only woman to hold the COO title for an MLB club.

Nineteen days later, the San Diego Padres announced the appointment of Caroline Perry to COO, making her the highest-ranking female executive in Padres history.

It is worth noting that two teams, the Seattle Mariners and the Miami Marlins, have women as President of Operations, leading the business side of the organization. Those two are Caroline O'Connor for the Marlins and Catie Griggs for the Mariners. This marks the first time women have had the top business-side jobs since 2008, when Jamie McCourt, who was also the wife of then Los Angeles Dodgers owner Frank McCourt, was the Dodgers' president and Pam Gardner held the same position with the Houston Astros.

Billy Bean serves as MLB's Senior Vice President of Diversity, Equity & Inclusion. According to the MLB website, as a senior advisor to Commissioner Rob Manfred he focuses on DE&I, player education, and social justice initiatives. Among his responsibilities, Bean leads all DE&I initiatives from the league office, as well as working with all thirty MLB clubs to foster an equitable, inclusive, and supportive workplace and baseball experience for everyone. On July 14, 2014, Bean was announced as Major League Baseball's first-ever Ambassador for Inclusion.

In a *Sports Business Journal* article, Bean pointed to the success of the Katy Feeney Leadership Symposium, among a handful of other DEI-focused initiatives, as reasons for the increase in women in MLB leadership positions. The symposium is designed to focus on career advancement for women in baseball and is held annually at the winter meetings.

"If we can get more of these dynamic, high-level women in positions such as general managers, assistant general managers, presidents, presidents of business operations, CEOs it starts to show something that people can believe in," Bean said. The more that can be seen the more interest will be promoted for all females.

"I'm hopeful that we're going to see the trend continue," Dodgers COO Caroline Perry said, "until it becomes a non-story when a woman gets one of those top senior positions." This is a common theme with women coaches and now, women leadership.

Major League Baseball and sports entities everywhere celebrate, every year, National Girls & Women in Sports Day. It is a day dedicated to recognizing the trailblazing women coaching on the field, and behind the scenes in the front office.

As part of this celebration, MLB hosts a group of college-age women at educational workshops, panels, and networking sessions with employees of the Commissioner's office, major league and minor league clubs, in an attempt to develop the next generation of powerful women in baseball.

Rangers Youth Academy coach Gigi Garcia, describing the speakers and panelists at the February 2024 celebration, "These amazing women are paving the way into the world of baseball, impacting the sport just like the women who started the first Girls Professional Baseball League in 1943. To be a successful woman in the industry, she learned that you must 'Be a visionary thinker, be comfortable with the uncomfortable, be open-minded and speak up and be uniquely you.'"

While MLB continues to create and implement inclusion programs to foster the advancement of women, ultimately it must happen through the initiative of the clubs.

Milwaukee Brewers COO Marti Wronski said it best, stating these inclusion efforts are not about just hiring or hitting some gender quota but leveling the perception of women in the sport, showing them in leadership roles, and eliminating gender bias. It was nice to hear her use the word "leveling" in her description. That's what *Leveling the Playing Field* encompasses and captures.

The stories and in-depth profiles of these successful women, their paths, skills, goals, and advice, are similar to those of women coaches. They offer a perspective on the experiences and background needed to get to a front office position, a rundown of the many twists and turns encountered along the way, how to handle gender issues, and advice to others who aspire to these positions. These women were unavailable for personal interviews, but other sources tell their stories. The following section will high-light just a few.

Kim Ng—A Unique Journey to a Pinnacle

Here we will review a unique journey, the important role women have in Major League Baseball today, and how diversity and inclusion in the sport's future are paramount.

Kim Ng rose to the pinnacle of a major league team when she became the general manager of the Miami Mar-lins. The headlines were many, but one that stood out was that, "We aren't in the 1950s anymore," meaning that we are no longer in the days when only men could lead an MLB club. Along the way, she had other significant roles, showing a break in the previous gender barriers where her jobs were formerly held by men. She has since left her pinnacle-level general management job, parting ways with the organization when she declined her 2024 mutual option (in which either party can choose to stay or leave). She blazed a trail and for that she is important as we understand and explore the growing role of women in MLB management.

Ng came to the Marlins with vast experience, having worked in front office leadership roles with the White Sox (1990-96), Yankees (1998-2001) and Dodgers (2002-11)—winning three World Series championships—before moving on to the commissioner's office, where she had worked since leaving the Dodgers in 2011.

All of these accomplishments are really no surprise.

A 2003 *Sports Illustrated* cover story ranked Ng close to the top third of its list of 101 Most Influential Minorities in Sports. The magazine, in prognosticating fashion, told us all at that time, "Write it down: Ng may become baseball's first female GM." Seventeen years later in 2020, that prediction finally came true. She made history by becoming the general manager of the Marlins, the highest-ranking woman in baseball operations among the thirty teams and the first woman general manager of any North American professional men's team.

The message sent was that she was an amazing hire, highly competent and qualified, had over thirty years of experience in baseball, and was a very good leader. Notice that there is no mention of gender. Sure, the headlines were present upon her hiring but underlying all of them was her role as a general manager, not a female general manager. That would be the epitome of fairness in her appointment.

Kim Ng has been a trailblazer and an inspiration in the evolving landscape of baseball, championing the game's progress toward inclusion.

Ng credits her father with encouraging her love of sports. From a baseball point of view, her passion was fired and driven by watching the New York Yankees of the late 70s. That passion carried her along her path into history.

Like many females, Ng grew up on a ball diamond playing softball in her younger years. She sums up the experience by saying, "I think I was the typical smaller, spunky player. I always had to have very good mechanics because of my size. But definitely always putting 110 percent effort out there, which is probably how you would describe my career as well. Never the biggest or the loudest in the room, but definitely always there before and after putting forth good effort and making the most of my ability." Lots of that quote holds true in each of her roles in Major League Baseball all the way up to her pinnacle general manager position.

That toughness and spunk comes in handy in dealing with any gender challenges thrown at her. She had this to say for herself in dealing with those: "I don't wake up in the morning and say 'I'm a woman; it's going to be a real problem today,'" Ng told the *New York Times* in 2002. "It's not hard. It's not easy. It's just different than what guys experience."

Ng further reflected on her time in the game when asked about pushback about the way being a woman or more a woman of Asian descent. "I think many of us face unconscious bias on a fairly regular basis. I will say that in this job I'm a lot higher profile, so I think a lot more people recognize me. And when that happens, people are understanding, and it registers. But again, going to the unconscious bias, it's not just me, it's many people in everyday life face it, whether you're in line at the grocery store or you're driving on the road, or you just come into contact with people who are not very kind. It can be a tough road if you let it bother you too much. But the fact of the matter is we still face it."

As women make progress in sports, they frequently encounter doubt about their capacity to lead, particularly in sports where they did not compete at a professional level themselves.

Ng, like many other women in male-dominated industries, would rather not be singled out for anything other than her work. While she does not actively seek the spotlight, Ng understands the significance of being a visible symbol of progress for many people.

Sports fans all over know a historic appointment like hers can and will change baseball for the better. The females in coaching and leadership roles know this and other appointments will improve their own career paths. Rachel Balkovec, now the Marlins' director of player development and the first woman hired as a Yankees hitting coach said, "It changes the conversation from, 'Oh it's never been done,' to, 'Oh, well, Kim's doing it so you can do it.'"

Other women noticed and publicly stated similar sentiments. Sara Goodrum, who at the time was director of player development for the Houston Astros and is now director of special projects for the Miami Marlins told MLB.com, "When I really started to process it was when Kim Ng got hired. For me, that hire really showed me somebody who I could finally, really, truly look up to. Someone who has made it to a pinnacle position in a Major League organization. It took me a moment to be, like, people could look at me like that. I think it motivated me more than anything to continue to want to make a positive impact in baseball and continue to push the needle forward in making the Brewers' player development unique."

Women noticed, the press noticed, the commissioner of baseball noticed, and they all spoke out in favor of Ng and her new role at the time. Looking back, former MLB commissioner Bud Selig was also on board, saying, "It is a barrier, that's fair to say, and I do think barriers are broken down, hopefully sooner rather than later." Selig practiced and believed in what he preached, as his daughter Wendy Selig-Prieb served for six years as CEO of the Milwaukee Brewers, the franchise Selig once owned.

Ng's successor as assistant general manager of the Yankees, Jean Afterman, said, "The barrier is broken when you find the right candidate regardless of gender. Now, in some cases, women have to be more qualified than the men."

Some people call it perseverance. Others call it knocking on doors consistently. This quote was all over upon her hiring by the Marlins. Ng said in a statement released by the team, "When I got into this business, it seemed unlikely a woman would lead a major league team, but I am dogged in the pursuit of my goals."

It is clear to see that Ng's persistence and steadfast belief in herself and her ability to lead, despite the long path to the pinnacle of her sport, is an example of the, "leveling the playing field attitude," in action.

Ng broke it down pretty simply when talking about the job she was hired for. It's worth noting her heartfelt feeling: "For the thirty of us that have these jobs, I think we feel a responsibility to the people that rely on us—to our staffs, to the players, and our organizations—to do everything that we can to make us better day in and day out."

The future for women in Major League Baseball is bright. Kim Ng says, "I think, particularly for women now in this industry, I believe it has gotten better. Together as a collective we're becoming not so much of a novelty where you don't just do a double take. We're not quite there yet, but we're working on it." Please, let's get to a point of no more double takes.

Marti Wronski—Local Girl Does Good

Local girl does good. That is, if local is the state of Wisconsin.

In December 2022, Marti Wronski was promoted to chief operating officer of the Milwaukee Brewers, making her the first woman in MLB to hold that title. Wronski was already familiar with the C-suite, having served as the Brewers' longtime general counsel. At that time, she was the organization's highest ranking female executive since the days of Wendy Selig-Prieb, when she held the position of president and chair of the board.

Anytime the words, "first woman" show up, that is progress for gender equality and in this case the sport of baseball.

As a lifelong athlete Wronski truly loves sports. Her family consists of four young sons and a Milwaukee native for a husband, so baseball becoming front and center in her world was not a strange event. Even while attending law school, Wronski was a serious athlete. After all, she is very comfortable in that environment, at work or at play.

In her previous position as general counsel, Wronski was involved in player contracts, licensing agreements, sponsor contracts, trademarks, and more. She also oversaw minor league affiliate legal affairs, information technology, and human resources.

Before taking on her role as chief operating officer, she was asked by the official publication of the state bar of Wisconsin, *Wisconsin Lawyer*, how important baseball knowledge was to her job even with her interest and athletic prowess. She said she had a very real understanding of what the employees and the team are working to accomplish, and she needed that understanding to deal with the many legal issues that came up. For things she doesn't have complete knowledge of, she learns by listening and finding the right people to ask the right questions of, plus reading and consuming a lot of information.

At the announcement of Wronski as COO, Brewers president of business operations Rick Schlesinger said, "Marti's promotion was based on merit, based on ability, judgment, and experience, not on gender. The reality in our profession is that women are not represented anywhere close to the numbers we'd like to see. That's the business side and the baseball side. We are all seeing that change for the good these days.

"If a young woman is looking to get into baseball, and they see somebody like Marti, maybe that will inspire them." In other words, seeing is believing for young women who wonder if there is a place for them in professional baseball.

By now Wronski has spent twenty years with the organization, so she knows her way around, despite gender. This experience raises hopes for other women in the sport to achieve the same type of longevity.

She knows few women were involved at the C-suite level in the past. She is also aware that this is changing. For those seeking similar positions, as females, she suggests, "Keep your nose down and work hard." We hear that advice coming from most other female coaches we've talked with. Wronski continues, "There is not necessarily any magic to attaining these positions. I really believe that if you work your tail off and you do it right, things will happen." She tells others that's how she got her opportunity.

Gender-related issues have not come in negative ways. She almost says her gender works in her favor because it makes her appear more approachable.

When talking to young women who want to get into baseball, she always encourages them to do so. She explains that it may take time to get what they want and patience can be a virtue. She goes on to talk about having the right skill set when they are ready to take a leap into the sport, though that advice applies to everyone, male or female.

Wronski has said publicly that her aim is to continue to champion women in sports, especially baseball and the Brewers. In a report by Adam McCalvy for MLB.com, Wronski said, "I've worked in a predominantly male sport, and I've had these awesome men and women that I've worked for where gender has not needed to be highlighted. I can't close my eyes and be ignorant to the fact that it is something unique." She went on to say, "What I'm most excited about is to sort of be part of this movement in the right direction. There is no doubt that right now in baseball, regardless of if it's the business or the baseball side, we're looking for the best and brightest talent."

Finally, she does talk of being honored and thrilled to be part of the movement toward female inclusion.

One more note: It's not certain if this has anything to do with helping females join the sport of Major League baseball or...maybe it does. Wronski is the surrogate mother of the Brewers' mascot dog, Hank, who the team rescued when he wandered into their spring training facility before the start of the 2014 season. Hank is now more of a pet than a mascot though he still makes appearances now and then.

Caroline O'Connor—Taking a logical step?

When a person's career spans high-profile roles with companies such as IBM, UBS Investment Bank and Morgan Stanley, what is the next most logical step? If you answered anything other than President of Business Operations for the Miami Marlins, you would be wrong. With the move to the Marlins, O'Connor became part of the growing class of females in executive and leadership roles in professional baseball.

O'Connor oversees all of the Marlins' business operations. These include sales, partnerships, marketing, analytics and strategy, human resources and diversity, finance, legal, communications, community outreach, technology, security, ballpark facilities, and special projects. Add to this her work in the outside world promoting her brand and building a community. David Oxfeld, chief commercial officer for the Marlins, said, "We need a face of the brand, and she is exactly that for us."

The chairman and principal owner of the Marlins, Bruce Sherman, has stated, "We are fortunate to have someone with Caroline's business acumen and vision leading our day-to-day business operations. Her passion and drive for success is unmatched in our game. Her leadership will continue to guide the Marlins organization toward our goal of sustained success while strategizing additional new ventures to grow our business and enhance our brand recognition." Sherman has also said O'Connor has a tireless work ethic and a command of the issues surrounding the business operations of a franchise.

Caroline O'Connor didn't come from a pro sports background. She did play her fair share growing up, including basketball, tennis, soccer, and softball, experiencing the thrill of competition and the ups and downs of sports. She worked in financial and management positions before making the transition to baseball and the Marlins. She blends people skills with the sense of structure that comes from growing up in a military household as the sixth of eight children and the daughter of a West Point graduate father.

O'Connor entered an organization that had its share of issues, and some even say crises. Kim Elsesser, senior contributor for *Forbes,* was quoted as saying, "The more feminine characteristics typically associated with female managers, like behaving in an understanding, intuitive and creative manner, may be more desirable in crises." So far, so good in dealing with so-called crises for O'Connor and the team.

The fact that O'Connor is in a very visible role is an understatement. She not only promotes her brand around the community, but is looked up to by others wanting to get into the business of baseball, especially females. She said her career trajectory is proof that there's a place in sports for everyone.

"When I talk to young girls, I really like them to see me in my role because I didn't feel like I had that role model," O'Connor told the *Associated Press.* "I want people to see themselves when they see me and know that it is a possibility."

O'Connor is a trailblazer, which she doesn't take lightly. "I take every chance I can to accept a LinkedIn request or if somebody I bump into wants to talk about their career aspirations or about how they can position themselves for a role like mine, I talk with them," she has said. "That's important to me."

Count, "role model for girls and women in sports," as one of the things that comes from O'Connor's accomplishments and her position with the Marlins.

As reported by CBS in a story on International Women's Day, O'Connor said, "It's absolutely for them. There's a place here for people just like me. I've been honored with a lot of the attention that I've gotten. But really, we go out and speak in the community, so those little girls see us and go 'I can do that one day'. I hope to inspire them and hope that they add it into their realm of possibilities of what they can do when they grow up."

Billy Bean of MLB, after asking O'Connor to speak at an MLB function (which she agreed to do), told *Sports Business Journal*, "This is what it takes to be a trailblazer. She's got a willingness to be a part of the process. I'm really looking to her to be an advocate for women to make the consideration for a career in baseball, because when she walks out there, with her title, knowing she's at the top, that's pretty powerful."

With all of our female coaches and leaders, we like to dig deep and understand how they fared with gender challenges and what their advice is for other women who want to enter baseball.

O'Connor's commitment to excellence and determination has paved the way for future generations of women to go after and obtain roles in the sports industry. As O'Connor herself says, "There's no excuse not to do your best every day." Clearly, she has taken her own sage advice, which is not only for girls and women but for men as well.

Caroline tells the story of being asked for a picture by a young female fan, whose father told how seeing her in the Marlins role meant a lot for his daughter. He said,

"This is Caroline. She's the president of the Miami Marlins. You could be this too."

Jean Afterman—Been there and doing that

Jean Afterman is the Assistant General Manager of the New York Yankees, following in the footsteps of Kim Ng, the first woman GM. Before joining the Yankees, Afterman worked as a player agent, representing several Japanese star players, including Hideki Irabu, Hideo Nomo, and Hideki Matsui. She has continued to excel in her role, collaborating closely with Brian Cashman, who holds the distinction of being the longest-tenured general manager in major league baseball.

Afterman says, "My job is sort of covering everything, and somebody in the business once said to me, 'Well, you are the glue.' I guess I am proud of being the glue." That meant she focuses on player contracts, rule compliance, and the club's business in Asia.

Afterman's responsibilities have expanded significantly beyond what her title might suggest. According to Cashman, she oversees business and legal affairs for baseball operations, which includes major and minor league affairs, international scouting, and foreign operations.

In 2019, Baseball America recognized her with the "Trailblazer" award for her efforts in paving the way for women in baseball front offices. Her contributions and leadership have consistently earned acclaim throughout her career.

She will say that she was always a baseball fan, spending lots of time in the bleachers in Candlestick Park in San Francisco as a child. She was interested in the game at that point but not what one would consider passionate. Her passions led her on different non-baseball paths that eventually brought her into the business and legal aspects of the game.

"To say that the gender aspect doesn't matter is naive," Afterman said in a UC Berkley alumni publication. "But in any situation where you're the other, you have to find your own way of dealing with that." The publication reported that she took the direct approach and trained Cashman, her boss, to introduce her as the assistant general manager. "He even does me the service of saying 'Be careful, she's a pit bull attorney!' But truly, if he does say 'this is my assistant'—then it's all about getting coffee and typing letters."

Afterman has said, "I am grateful every day—not only that I have a job, but that I'm working for the Yankees. It's an organization that doesn't stand still. Some organizations are mired in their history and tradition, and they can't move forward, and the Yankees certainly move forward. It is a privilege to serve Rome," or in other words, at the pinnacle of baseball.

Gene Orza, the former associate general counsel and chief operating officer of the MLB Players Association, said, "She helped reduce the lack of affinity for females in the sport that is harbored by still some people in high places. The Yankees kept an eye on her. They spotted her talent. Then they wanted to hire her. It was a smart move."

Growing up in Presidio Heights, California, Jean Afterman never considered her gender a potential barrier. Her father, a psychoanalyst, and her mother, Marjorie, who later earned a master's degree after being a stay-at-home mom, taught her and her three brothers to always stand up for what is right and to rely on their intellect to achieve their dreams. Queen Elizabeth I, known for her strong will, was Afterman's childhood hero, leading her to believe that if a woman could rule England in the 16th century, women could succeed in a man's world today.

Afterman draws parallels to her own experiences, recognizing herself as a woman in a traditionally male-dominated domain. Aware of the lack of representation for women in baseball, Afterman acknowledges the importance of visibility and opportunity. Early on, she served as a beacon for women aspiring to careers on the baseball side, striving to expand the talent pool for interested clubs through collaboration with the league.

While Afterman acknowledges she won't be the first female general manager in MLB (that was Kim Ng), she remains enthusiastic about paving the way for future female leaders. She sees the placement of women in prestigious executive roles as crucial, emphasizing the responsibility she and other high-profile women have to advocate for themselves and their achievements.

In an interview with *LEADERS Magazine*, Afterman stresses that success in professional sports is determined by merit rather than gender. However, she also highlights the systemic barriers that limit women's opportunities, calling for change to ensure equality of opportunity.

Eve Rosenbaum—Coming Home to a Dream Job

Landing the dream job with the team she grew up watching. That sums up Eve Rosenbaum and her role as Assistant General Manager of the Baltimore Orioles.

With Kim Ng's departure as GM of the Marlins, Eve's position ranks highest among women in MLB. Her job entails handling the day-to-day operations of a major league team. She followed a crazy, somewhat non-baseball path but she landed in the right place.

Eve Rosenbaum's passion for baseball and the Orioles began when she was growing up. She estimates she went to over seventy games a year, thanks to her parents having season tickets for the whole family. She wanted to work in sports in one capacity or another but wasn't sure what that would look like going forward. However, she was destined for a baseball life. At her bat mitzvah, her cake was in the shape of an iced baseball.

She knew a good education would be a foundation for her. She relied on her education, in her case from Harvard, for the development of critical thinking, communication, and general life skills, all useful in any leadership position including, assistant general manager of a major league team.

Here is what she said about that in an interview with MLB's Mark Feinsand: "Baseball is so all-consuming. I just found it fascinating; with psychology, you're talking about how people think, how people behave and what their motivations are. That actually comes into play a lot in baseball."

Now about her non-baseball path: After graduating from Harvard, Eve went to work for the National Football League. From an entry-level job, she was promoted to manager of business intelligence and optimization. Not a lot of sports people have that title, and she wasn't sure where it would lead, but she wanted to be in sports. She considered that experience very valuable as she learned firsthand about running a team as a business and all the inside details. Before joining the NFL, Eve interned for the Boston Red Sox and the MLB executive office. But still, exactly how did football lead to baseball?

As Mark Feinsand reported, Eve got a message from Oz Campo, who was in international operations with the Houston Astros and working on a joint project with Eve in her NFL job. His message said, "I'm now the international scouting director for the Astros and I'm looking to hire someone to help me. I remember that you were really good, and you were very passionate about baseball. Would you have any interest in coming to work here?"

At first Eve wondered why she would disrupt her current good situation, but then realized the position could be a once-in-a-lifetime chance to jump into baseball. Fast forward to the beginning of 2015 when Eve got the Astros job. She was now in baseball and quickly got promoted to manager of international scouting.

After five years with the Astros, Eve joined Orioles general manager Mike Elias as the director of baseball development, responsible for developing and implementing evaluation methods and digital analytics for all baseball operations. She was the conduit between the organization's scouting, player development, and R & D departments. Eve called her return to Baltimore a homecoming, a dream job, and one she described as, "surreal."

Similar to what we've heard from all the other women coaches and front office leaders, thinking about working in baseball "as a female," is not her way. Eve told Mark Feinsand she was just doing her job and was focused on getting the team to the playoffs. "I'm not thinking, 'I'm Eve, the fourth woman AGM ever and I have a spotlight on me, so I have to take that in consideration with everything that I do.' I don't think that way because I've always been me. I wake up in the morning, here's my job and that's what I'm going to do."

Eve knows, however, that people still think about the gender barrier being broken. She does reflect on the fact of overcoming gender challenges, and what that means to younger women that might have baseball aspirations. She knows it's valuable that they see her in a leadership position.

For a much of Eve's career, there were not a lot of women in baseball or football. That left her to drive on, do the job at hand and accomplish team goals of winning and championships. She continually states that she doesn't give much thought to her gender status; after all, she did play on boys' teams during her Baltimore-area upbringing.

Whether in baseball or soccer, being the only girl on an all-boys team was just part of who she was.

Eve says her personality allows her to have a positive experience being a woman in a field dominated by men.

Eve talks about how being able to get along with any and all types of people is an asset in her job. She also considers herself to be resourceful, able to handle anything that comes her way.

Besides gender interference, there is general pushback by fans. Fans either hate a general manager's move, or in this case an assistant general manager's move, or they love it. Eve knows what her job is, why she has it, and the overall goal. Fans have opinions but don't know the inner workings and information available to those making team decisions. Separating out fans' opinions from the work at hand and the reasons for it is something that has to be done. Eve says sports is a very public job and an assistant general manager's work can be visible to all.

In a Q & A session with the *Baltimore Jewish Times*, Eve was asked if it was difficult to work as a woman in the sports industry. Her response: "Fortunately, I haven't really had any difficulties. It was only within the past handful of years that I was able to sort of reflect and be like, 'Wow, I've been doing all this as a woman.' But I've worked with a really good set of men, my coworkers from the NFL and Major League Baseball. They've never once made me feel like I'm the woman in the room. They just make me feel like I'm part of a team, and they value my opinions. So,

I think that's a huge aspect, is having the support of the people around you."

Eve will deal with whatever comes her way next. Her fingerprints are already all over the work that general manager Elias is directing.

As Eve says, her whole story is surreal. Coming home to the Orioles has been described as icing on the cake of her career. She is now where many women who want to work in baseball dream of being, working where she watched games as a child, coming back, and rooting for her hometown team. Eve loves seeing the Orioles brand represented all over her city and the major leagues, while she thinks to herself, "I'm doing that. I'm part of that."

VII. Voices of Change

Male Advocates for Women in Baseball Coaching and Management

———

Baseball, often dubbed "America's pastime," has traditionally been a male-dominated sport both on and off the field. It has produced role models and idols, created millionaires, and bestowed celebrity status upon individuals. Baseball's influence is profound, evoking strong emotions and discussions. While we often hear about boys dreaming of becoming baseball stars, we overlook the girls who are equally exposed to the sport's glorification but not encouraged to play. As younger generations challenge gender stereotypes, female athletes are asserting their prowess to secure the same opportunities as their male counterparts. For over a century and until recent years, roles such as general managers, assistant coaches, and rostered players in baseball were exclusively held by men. Figures like Kim

Ng, Alyssa Nakken, and Rachel Balkovec have broken barriers and made history as some of the first women recognized for their success in coaching and management.

The debate over female athletes participating in men's sports continues, but with the progress made and the increasing recognition of women's achievements in baseball, it may not be a debate for much longer. While some of this has been covered in each coach's section, much of it bears repeating or being added to.

Early in Ronnie Gajownik's career with the Arizona Diamondbacks, manager Torey Lovullo asked her to sit with him during a game against the Western Division rival San Diego Padres. Although this was a training exercise, Lovullo thought enough of Gajownik to ask her to be his bench coach in the game. For nine innings they watched every play and talked in detail about ideas and strategy. Again, this was a major compliment to the up-and-coming Gajownik and t was coming from the manager himself.

Lovullo has publicly voiced his support of Gajownik and all of her work. He appreciated the nine innings he spent on the bench with her dissecting the game and has high regards for her demeanor, approach, and how she relates to players.

Lovullo has stated, "I've been in baseball a long time, and unfortunately, it's taken the game this long to get this far, but it's moving very quickly in the right direction and I'm happy about it. There have been a lot of pioneers out there, and to all those women that have taken chances that have given Ronnie this opportunity, I commend them."

Ronnie did step back and reflect on her experience with Lovullo, saying she is grateful and that her pioneering is starting to sink in.

Experiences like this are happening around the league, although not being publicized. Many of the comments at the time of women's hiring are compliments for them and praise for the gender barrier being broken.

This was stated in the section about Sara Goodrum but it's worth retelling because of its importance as it relates to gender. Said Tom Flanagan, the Brewers farm director at the time of Sara's promotion, "I think gender is really a non-issue, where we're at today in the game. Specifically, with Sara, there is a familiarity with our hitters. She has been around the batting cage for the last couple of years, so there are relationships there, there's knowledge of what we're trying to do and what she's trying to do."

Before Bianca Smith's professional career, she was Case Western Reserve University's first baseball operations manager. Coach Matt Englander, who hired her, expounded, "She deserved a chance because she was so smart and passionate and probably loves the sport more than I do."

David Bell, the manager of the Cincinnati Reds said this about Smith, "Bianca could walk into a major league staff right now and contribute. There is no doubt in my mind about that. I really believe that she is capable of doing anything in this game."

Both statements were directly about Smith and her abilities. At no time did gender come up in those comments, nor in the two men's thinking.

Veronica Alvarez, the esteemed female coach for the Oakland Athletics, has been extensively discussed in the media. Like other highly-praised hires, Alvarez is a strategic fit for the Athletics organization. That has been substantiated by assistant GM Dan Feinstein, whose called her the perfect fit. Feinstein raved about her high-level passion, enthusiasm, and energy as well as her knowledge and ability to relate to players, staff, and coaches in the organization.

When Gretchen Aucoin played for the Bussolengo club in Verona, Italy as part of the Italian season for the Olympic qualifiers, she received a worthy endorsement from a male coach. Craig Montvidas, an American, complimented Aucoin on being very disciplined. Discipline leads to professionalism, and he said she was one of the most professional players he had coached, including more than twenty Olympic athletes. He went on to say, "Coaching would be very simple if all players were like her." Again, nothing was said about being female or gender inclusion. It was about Aucoin as a player in that case and the qualities that carried through to her professional coaching career.

Alyssa Nakken is often spoken of as the prominent trailblazer in her MLB coaching career. She had been classified as a baseball coach, not a female baseball coach.

According to an article, by John Shea, the *San Francisco Chronicle's* national baseball writer and columnist, Giants general manager Pete Putila had this to say about Nakken, "Generally speaking, she's really good at building relationships, not only with staff but the players, and bringing people together and organizing things, whether it's meetings or action from meetings. She wears a lot of different hats in addition to on-field coaching, so she's definitely a valuable resource for the Giants." He added, "She's an inspiration for a lot of women wanting to get into the game, whether it's in coaching or other roles around baseball. With the Giants, she's a great connector and really good at identifying opportunities where we can make improvements on the field or in an office environment."

When Kim Ng was named general manager of the Miami Marlins, Commissioner Rob Manfred said, "Kim's appointment makes history in all of professional sports and sets a significant example for the millions of women and girls who love baseball and softball. The hard work, leadership, and record of achievement throughout her long career in the national pastime led to this outcome, and we wish Kim all the best as she begins her career with the Marlins." We can only hope there are more women general managers selected for Manfred to comment on, and coaching slots for other qualified females growing at a quicker pace.

In the summer of 2021 LaTroy Hawkins, a former big-league reliever, was managing the Futures Game put on by MLB. Hawkins stated that when hiring coaches for the annual event, he was blown away by Rachel Balkovec's resume. He thought she was she was beyond qualified for a hitting coach job, and it was well past time for a woman to be a part of the game, which showcases minor leaguers during that year's MLB's All-Star Weekend.

"When she walked in, she was immediately ready to do the job," the former Yankees and Mets reliever said. "She not only had the breakdown on the players on the other team, but on our team. She was confident. She was bilingual. She was able to communicate with the players.

"She is so prepared, she is ready," Hawkins said. "I am so glad to see her get her chance."

Lastly, when asked about whether women could make it to the major leagues, whether playing, coaching, or managing, experts offer positive opinions.

Mike Scioscia, who spent thirty-two years in the majors as a manager and All-Star catcher with the Angels and Dodgers, told the Los Angeles Times, "Yeah, I think it's a definite possibility."

Commissioner Manfred has publicly said, "Women playing baseball is an important part of our sport's history." Where that philosophy goes, no one can say, but it illustrates how the gender barrier has broken.

With all these comments from male managers, coaches and participants in Major League Baseball, success for these women is at hand. Paying attention to the person, not necessarily just the gender is major progress in inclusion.

Insight from those within MLB

In a report for MLB by sports columnist Paul Hagen in 2015, Commissioner Manfred reiterated baseball's commitment to creating opportunities for women and minorities. This happened on the final day of the 2015 Sports Diversity & Inclusion Symposium held that year at Citi Field.

Manfred's comments continued to stress that MLB feels strongly that diversity is the right thing to do.

"You can't just say, 'I'm going to improve my employment statistics' and rest on that as your diversity program in today's world,'" he said. "Our people want to do the right thing. But it's much easier to get people committed to doing the right thing when your programs are supportive of your fundamental business objectives."

Manfred noted that MLB has invested over $1 billion with minority and female-owned businesses. He said, "That's in addition to the money being spent on programs like the Urban Youth Academies, Elite Development Invitational, Play Ball initiative and the RBI (Reviving Baseball in Inner Cities) and the $30 million partnership with the Major League Baseball Players Association which are all designed to attract minority athletes to the game."

The hope is that the best athletes will eventually play and coach in the big leagues and others will continue to follow the game as fans. The Commissioner also mentioned the efforts being made to recruit minorities for positions of authority both on and off the field, (including coaching). "The other thing we're doing is very actively engaging with the clubs and focusing in the Commissioner's Office on entry-level positions. I think it's important not to just think about GMs and field managers but, over the long haul, to focus on the pool of people who ultimately will mature into candidates for those senior leadership positions."

Years later (2022), the Commissioner said, "We are committed to ensuring any young woman who chooses to play baseball…will have the opportunity to do so."

Usually when anything historic happens for MLB, the Commissioner will speak up. The comments are straightforward but many times worth noting. The hiring of Rachel Balkovec as the first woman to be a full-time hitting coach and the first woman manager in the history of affiliated professional baseball was such an occasion: "On behalf of Major League Baseball, I congratulate Rachel on this historic milestone. As manager of the Tampa Tarpons, she will continue to demonstrate her expertise and leadership in the Yankees organization. We wish Rachel well in this new capacity and appreciate her mentorship to the growing network of women in baseball operations and player development roles. (Reported in January 2022 by Kristie Ackert, *New York Daily News Tribune News Service*).

These voices of change sound loud and mostly proud. The legacy of these voices will be the increasing numbers of women coaches and females in baseball front office leadership.

VIII. Plans and Views of Success

MLB's Commitment—Efforts, Initiatives and Programs to Foster Inclusivity

M ajor League Baseball knows the league is still overwhelmingly white and male at the managerial, front office, and coaching levels. People of color and women have found it hard to break through, but the situation is improving.

To further this improvement, MLB has many proactive initiatives addressing inclusion concerns. While much of the talk of inclusion and diversity centers around players, managers, and leaders of color, this section will focus on women, in light of their increasing numbers. More women hold major or minor league coaching jobs than ever before, including player development positions.

One of the most proactive measures an organization can take is to appoint an organization diversity and inclusion head, someone responsible for monitoring and enforcing standards. Billy Bean serves at MLB as senior vice president of diversity, equity, and inclusion (DE&I). As a senior advisor to the commissioner, his role focuses on DE&I, player education, and social justice initiatives. According to MLB, Bean's responsibilities include leading all DE&I initiatives from the league office, as well as working with all thirty MLB clubs to foster an equitable, inclusive, and supportive workplace and baseball experience for everyone. In July of 2014, Bean was announced as baseball's first-ever Ambassador for Inclusion.

Much has been written about Kim Ng, a trailblazer at leveling the playing field, who has been at the forefront of the ever-changing world of baseball as the game has advanced in its efforts toward inclusion. She had this to say as a guest on the National Baseball Hall of Fame and Museum's *Voice of the Game* series, a program put on in conjunction with the National Archives Foundation: "I think Major League Baseball has done a nice job of providing opportunity and access for the young women and girls that do have profound, deep interest in the game. And so, you're not just providing opportunity, but really trying to help develop these young women and girls and connecting them to different Major League clubs to provide a training ground for them. I've been really happy with a lot of their formal programming that they've done over the last five years."

MLB has worked to diversify in many ways. Ng's hiring is one example and the many coaches described herein represent others. This is progress but still considered limited. In what MLB says is a top-down cultural shift in its workplace attitude toward women, the league has launched employee networks such as the MLB Women Business Resource Group and the many others described below.

It was stated earlier but it's worth re-stating, "Women playing baseball is an important part of our sport's history," according to Commissioner Rob Manfred. "That legacy is also significant to the game's present and future. We are proud to work alongside USA Baseball in creating events that raise the profile of girls and women baseball." Manfred's comments also go toward women playing baseball, "We are committed to ensuring that any young woman who chooses to play baseball, particularly through our RBI programs and MLB Youth Academies, will have the opportunity to do so."

MLB has this diversity, equity and inclusion mission:

> *To support and sustain a diverse and inclusive culture, on and off the field, the power of our collective creates a meaningful experience for our people, our fans, and our communities. We strive to provide a rewarding and prosperous environment for our employees, to be the sport of choice for a diverse and growing fan base, and to be a responsible steward of our communities. (Source: Mlb.com)*

Diversity, Equity, and Inclusion Pillars

That MLB DE&I mission and vision is based on these pillars:

- **PEOPLE:** Our success is inherent in the diversity of our personnel, alongside our ability to recruit, develop, retain, promote, and support each other.
- **CULTURE:** Our commitment to empowering an inclusive environment built on acceptance, awareness, belonging, communication, leadership, and respect.
- **COMMUNITY:** Our promise to use the power and character of our sport to strengthen the communities where we live, work and play.

Much of the following information is from mlb.com, in particular the DE&I pages. Some of these programs go beyond gender inclusion and include other minorities and young boys. However, many still focus on female inclusion.

MLB's Employee Resource Groups

In 2017, the MLB Central Office launched its Employee Resource Groups (ERG). These are voluntary, employee-led groups whose aim is to foster a sense of camaraderie, community, and learning, alongside a diverse and inclusive workplace that aligns with the values of the sport.

The one focused on here is the MLB Women group, whose mission is to cultivate an inclusive environment that inspires women to advance their leadership potential through networking, mentorship, and collaboration. The group strives to inspire women to succeed and excel both professionally and personally.

Other Employee Resource Groups include:
- Military Veteran Professionals
- Somos for the Latino community
- MLB Pride
- Hype: Helping Young Professionals Excel
- MLB Home Base: Work-life balance
- MLB Black
- Asian Employee Resource Group
- Athletes to Executives

MLB Diversity Fellowship Program

The MLB Diversity Fellowship Program was created to expand the talent pool of future baseball leaders. The program provides the opportunity for early-career professionals to experience front office positions that have traditionally been influential in baseball operations decisions. This opportunity places candidates in entry-level roles in participating clubs and MLB's League office for eighteen to twenty-four months.

National Girls & Women in Sports Day

As part of a 2024 National Girls & Women in Sports Day event, there was, as MLB stated, a celebration of equal opportunity, a day dedicated to recognizing the trailblazing women on the playing surface and behind the scenes. MLB annually hosts a group of college-age women to attend educational workshops, panels, and networking sessions with employees of the Commissioner's office, as well as individual major and minor league teams, to develop the next generation of powerful women in the industry.

Former Youth Academy athlete turned part-time coach for the Rangers Youth Academy Gigi Garcia had this to say about the speakers and panelists at the Sports Day celebration: "These amazing women are paving the way into the world of baseball, impacting the sport just like the women who started the first Girls Professional Baseball League in 1943." To be a successful woman in the industry, she learned that one must, "Be a visionary thinker, be comfortable with the uncomfortable, be open-minded and speak up and be uniquely you."

Katy Feeney Leadership Awards

The Katy Feeney Leadership Awards are an annual program that recognizes one exceptional female employee in the front office at each of the thirty teams, one from the Office of the Commissioner, and one from the MLB Network. This prestigious award is designed to celebrate the significant contributions and outstanding initiative demonstrated by these women and to honor the legacy of Katy Feeney, whose pioneering leadership, accomplishments, and influence have left an indelible mark on the game.

From Wikipedia: Katy Feeney was a Major League Baseball executive for forty years under six commissioners, retiring as senior vice president of club relations and scheduling. Few women reached her level in the ranks. She was the daughter of longtime baseball executive Chub Feeney.

Take the Field

Take the Field is a two-day event at the annual winter meetings specifically designed for women interested in front office and on-field baseball careers. Take the Field provides opportunities for education and engagement with club and league personnel through panels, breakout sessions, and professional development. MLB states:

> *The event offers an opportunity to learn from current baseball employees, develop in their areas of interest and network with their peers and other baseball professionals. Sessions focus on analytics, baseball operations, coaching, player development, replay, scouting and umpiring, as well as leadership, communication, and technology in baseball. Take the Field is helping more women find work in baseball.*

Diversity Pipeline Program

The Diversity Pipeline Program seeks to create experiential learning for applicants through various initiatives throughout the year, including a SABR analytics conference and the Diversity Pipeline Scout and Coaching Development Program.

The Diversity Pipeline Program was created by Commissioner Manfred in January 2016. Its goal is to identify and develop a broad spectrum of well-qualified candidates in baseball operations at all thirty teams and the Office of the Commissioner. Applicants will be considered for interviews for opportunities in player development (including athletic training and strength and conditioning), player evaluation/scouting, managing & coaching, baseball analytics, research and development, front office roles, and umpiring.

MLB Breakthrough Series

The Breakthrough Series provides girls an opportunity to improve their craft and learn valuable lessons both on and off the diamond. Female players receive high-level coaching. Those lessons have helped pave the path for women in MLB, whether as coaches or in the front office.

Veronica Alvarez, whose path was discussed earlier in this book, said this about a recent breakthrough series event: "The fact that these events exist just keeps providing opportunities for women in baseball to continue to grow and get better so that when we do get those opportunities in professional baseball, we crush it. There's no doubt that we belong."

MLB Dream Series

Major League Baseball and USA Baseball hosts the MLB Dream Series, a premier amateur baseball development camp developed to diversify the talent pool of minority pitchers and catchers. A recent event featured nearly eighty top Black and Latino high school players from across the nation. Athletes receive elite-level instruction from former major and minor league players, managers, and coaches.

Softball Elite Development Invitational

The Elite Development Invitational is a multi-day, eighteen-and-under training camp that features intense on-field softball development and game play along with various off-field development sessions covering topics such as college recruiting, mental health, and women in sports.

The event is coached by current and former USA Softball Women's National Team athletes, professional softball players, and college coaches. Participants represent some of the top athletes from the MLB Youth Academy and Nike RBI network.

MLB Grit

The MLB GRIT: Girls ID Tour is designed specifically for young female athletes (eighteen and under) to showcase their ability as baseball players. The event format is similar to a pro-style workout where athletes are evaluated on their talent. The top performers will be selected to participate in the Girls Baseball Elite Development Invitational, a one-week program geared toward providing elite training and instruction, as well as the annual Girls Baseball Breakthrough Series.

MLB Trailblazer Series

In 2017, USA Baseball and Major League Baseball launched a new baseball tournament for girls built around Jackie Robinson Day in celebration of baseball's quintessential "trailblazer." As part of the MLB Youth Development Events, the objective is to provide playing, development, and educational opportunities to girls who play baseball.

MLB Tour

Another Youth Development event is the MLB Tour, a grassroots initiative to identify talent in the graduating classes of 2027 and 2028 for baseball development programming.

MLB States Play

States Play is a premier high school baseball tournament run by MLB and USA Baseball, with the goal of showcasing some of the best underclass players from around the country. The vast majority of them have already verbally committed to some of the nation's top collegiate baseball programs. Former major league players and personnel serve as coaches for each squad.

MLB The Program

The Program consists of participation in baseball development activities each week from mid-June through mid-July, preparing participants for premier sixteen-and-under tournaments on weekends against some of the top travel programs from around the country.

The coaching staff is comprised of several former major leaguers who have been instructors for different development programs (Breakthrough Series, DREAM Series, States Play, etc.).

MLB Urban Youth Academy

Major League Baseball's first Urban Youth Academy was founded in 2006 in Compton, California. As a not-for-profit organization, the UYA aims to set the standard for baseball and softball instruction, teach and educate in urban America, and enhance the quality of life in the surrounding communities.

MLB Allyship

Allyship is a vital strategic tool employed by individuals to actively collaborate, support, and advocate for justice and equity in the workplace. It involves fostering personal relationships and engaging in public acts of sponsorship. Allies work toward systemic improvements in policies, practices, and culture. MLB encourages at all levels to continue to push diversity, equity, and inclusion forward.

Unfiltered Series

Unfiltered is a speaker series of D&I-focused topics designed to bring awareness, education, and information in a candid, truth-telling manner.

As seen from these many programs, MLB is now more serious about diversity and inclusion than ever before. The league states this seriousness directly on its website as it relates to the Legacy of Their Fellowship program, an effort to recruit the most talented individuals and brightest young minds for influential front office positions. As fellows, these diverse professionals will have the opportunity to learn baseball operations and see the inner workings of a front office.

> *"Baseball is a game that is played globally, featuring players whose backgrounds differ tremendously. Collectively, they compose a population as diverse as any other group of athletes in professional sport.*
>
> *Success on the field is not measured by one individual's talent, but rather how a team of individuals with different skills comes together to achieve a common goal. Each and every day, teams seek the best talent in order to stay ahead of the curve in the ultra-competitive landscape of the Major Leagues.*
>
> *Major League Baseball understands that we must apply that same approach to our front offices in order to secure the game's next generation of leadership."*

IX. Women in Baseball
What's Next

———

For any trend or movement there is always the question of what's next. The answers ensure that whatever is causing the trend is more of a movement and not just a moment. That question is appropriate here.

We've heard of the paths, the challenges, the different ways challenges and pushbacks were overcome, and advice for the next generation. Now it's time to learn from all of that and put that advice into action for all females, young and old and for all related organizations.

The future of gender equality, diversity, and inclusion depends on the collective efforts of individuals, communities, teams, leagues, and other organizations. It will require steadfast commitment, education, and untiring advocacy to shape a world of baseball that is truly inclusive, equitable and diverse for all.

We have also heard many wishes and visions, whether individual or organizational. Next is transforming visions into reality. Addressing gender inclusion must remain a priority.

Challenging what is normal, and the stereotypes of gender roles, is crucial to equity and inclusion in baseball. That is exactly what every coach and leader profiled here has done.

Many of those profiled speak often, publicly, loud and clear, about their journeys, their challenges, and their successes. The more female coaches and front office women in baseball that share and speak up, the more messages will be heard by all. That must continue.

The words, "must continue," will be a common theme when discussing, "What's next?" Yes, actions are to be imperative to contribute. That is part of what's next. The easy way would be to keep doing what has been done in the past but be cautious of becoming complacent. The risk is that complacency slows progress. Proactivity speeds it up.

Earlier it was mentioned that collective efforts of individuals, communities, teams, leagues, and other organizations will direct the future of gender inclusion in baseball. While there is much more to say about the following programs and organizations, let's take a look at highlights of the efforts.

Women in Baseball Events /Women in Baseball Week

There are many events related to women in baseball with a national profile and many more with a local profile. The highlight and primary showcase for women in baseball is the outright Women in Baseball Week.

From womeninbaseballweek.org:

> *Women in Baseball Week is an annual, worldwide event recognizing the value, diversity, and cultural significance of women in baseball. Women play a vital role in all aspects of the sport north, south, east, and west—-help us celebrate each one! Tournaments, teams, libraries, museums, and individuals will join the International Women's Baseball Center to recognize women's contributions to baseball around the globe.*

Also from the site: "While recent years have seen more women on the field, behind the plate, and in the broadcast booth, this momentum can only be sustained with everyone's investment in working together, all around the world. By joining forces and supporting those with similar goals, we create more opportunities, expand youth participation, and encourage a culture that places women at the center of the world's best sport."

Other Women in Baseball Week events of note include the All-American Women's Baseball Classic tournament put on by the American Girls Baseball organization (AGB). The event features non-stop baseball, hotly contested games, and memories on the baseball diamond.

This all represents a chance to celebrate some of the dynamic, pioneering, trail-blazing women working to make baseball better.

Non-Profit Organizations

Baseball For All is one example of a girls' baseball 501(c)3 nonprofit that builds gender equity by creating opportunities for girls to play, coach, and lead. The organization is involved in many areas related to girls' baseball and how to grow the game across the country.

One thing it is known for is Baseball for All Nationals, the largest girls' baseball tournament in the United States. The tournament comprises players in over forty states and five countries competing in tournaments all over the U.S., organized by Baseball for All.

Founder and CEO Justine Siegal has estimated that roughly a thousand girls each year are given an opportunity to play. As Siegal says, "Offer it and they will take it."

Playing College Baseball

College baseball programs all over the country report more women than ever are playing. A record number suited up for men's teams at various collegiate levels in the 2024 season and more are on the way. It truly is a movement to make women's baseball a college sport or at least make women part of men's teams. and it is gaining momentum. The more women playing, the more interest will be cultivated and increase coaching and front office jobs.

International

Throughout the world, women and girls have a rich history of participating in baseball, yet men and boys typically receive more opportunities to play. In Japan, Canada, and beyond, efforts by players and advocates are expanding the women's game at all levels. Their triumphs and challenges provide valuable insights for enhancing inclusivity in baseball within the United States.

However, around the world there are individuals striving to alter this pattern by expanding the game for a gender that has long been neglected. Unlike other countries, USA Baseball lacks state or regional-level leagues or competitions. Instead, it collaborates directly with Major League Baseball to organize events for young female athletes. These include the Trailblazer Series (ages 10-13), the Grit Girls Identification Tour (for high school baseball players), and the Breakthrough Series (ages 14-18).

Beyond USA Baseball, there are all-girls teams, including some that compete in travel leagues and tournaments. Similar efforts are needed in the United States to enhance the competitiveness of women's baseball globally and increase its worldwide audience.

Hiroko Yamada, a board member for the Baseball Federation of Japan, has discussed the possibility of establishing an international club championship. She believes competitive teams will elevate women's baseball to a higher standard.

USA Women's National Team

The Women's National Team secured a gold medal at the 2019 COPABE (Pan-American Baseball Confederation) women's Pan-American Championships, a remarkable achievement that led to them being honored with the 2019 USA Baseball Team of the Year Award.

When not participating in the World Cup, the team runs a Women's National Team Development Program. It also conducts youth clinics and contributes to the growth of baseball among women in the U.S. through collaborative efforts with MLB and USA Baseball. These initiatives include the Girls Breakthrough Series and Development Camp, the MLB GRIT Invitational, and the Trailblazer Series, all designed to nurture the next generation of female players.

All-American Girls Professional Baseball League Profile and Reunion

The All-American Girls Professional Baseball League Players Association is a non-profit organization dedicated to preserving the history of the league and supporting women and girls who deserve the opportunity to play baseball.

The organization is active, with a museum, articles on their website (aagpbl.org), and sponsored events.

American Girls Baseball

American Girls Baseball (AGB) benefits female baseball players and those who want to be in the game by providing opportunities to train, participate, and compete. AGB was created as an affiliate organization of the All-American

Girls' Professional Baseball League Players Association (AAGPBL PA) in 2019 to continue the legacy and purpose of this famous women's professional league.

- **Their vision:** A professional baseball league for girls and women who want to have a future in that sport.
- **Their purpose:** To benefit female baseball players who want to have a choice between softball and baseball and provide them with opportunities to train, participate, and compete in baseball at the high school, college, and professional levels.

International Women's Baseball Center

The International Women's Baseball center provides education and information to protect, preserve, and promote all aspects of women's baseball, both on and off the field. The center has a goal of inspiring the next generation of players. They do this by helping them realize their dreams of participating in the sport and pass on all that they learn and achieve for generations to come. This in effect is their stated mission, which they achieve with events, literary initiatives, and publishing information about women in baseball.

Minor League Baseball

With MiLB stating innovation and family-friendliness are its hallmarks, minor league teams are continually seeking ways to make their ballparks more welcoming and fun for girls and women.

Numerous teams are honoring women baseball pioneers each season, with events at local ballparks across the country. These efforts build on a tradition of promotions aimed at empowering women and girls in sports, coaching, the front office, and beyond.

The Atlantic League

Several female players have found success in the Atlantic League, one of the more prestigious independent leagues in North America. For Kelsie Whitmore, a pitcher and utility player for the (Staten Island) Ferry Hawks, it represented a chance to be the first woman to start a game in the league. Whitmore is not the last woman playing on the men's team. Her presence is viewed around the league and around baseball as putting her among the trailblazers who lead more women into the game.

Women in College Baseball

A rising number of women are playing on men's college baseball teams At the time of this writing, at least eight women across four divisions in the U.S. and Canada are on varsity rosters. More graduating high school seniors (in the class of 2024) have already committed to play for men's programs next season. Again, the more women become visible in situations like this, the more women will get involved.

Other Positions in MLB Organizations

Major League Baseball's mission and vision to provide diverse employment goes beyond coaching, the front office, and management to hiring them for other positions. Many times, females occupy the roles of strength and conditioning coach, broadcaster, on-air analysis, analytics, video, and more. As the diversity goals approach 50/50 or more, the more visible and attractive MLB employment becomes.

MLB Website

One thing that can be next is finding those jobs for women within MLB directly. MLB offers a career-oriented web page (mlb.com/careers/home) to help women find jobs. The page has tabs for each of the following categories: League Opportunities, MLB Team Opportunities, MiLB Team Opportunities, Programs, Locations, and Diversity & Inclusion.

Champions Throughout the Game

We have discussed, at length female coaching pioneers and female front office pioneers. Pioneers or champions of females in baseball can come from outside the league. Champions throughout the game will further the cause of females in Major League Baseball.

One of these champions is Jean Fruth, a baseball photographer and as she says, a visual storyteller. A favorite quote is, "I've learned that the game is more than just a sport—it is dreams and aspirations for so many youngsters everywhere I go. The culture of baseball is so much bigger than just what happens on the field."

Jean Fruth goes beyond taking great pictures. With a diverse portfolio in portraiture and sports of all kinds, Jean is devoted to capturing the dynamism of her subjects and revealing the stories behind the images—of colorful personalities, local cultures, and distinctive communities. Much of what she does is centered around females in baseball. The game can always use champions like Jean.

As all of these programs continue and more events occur, the state of females in baseball will continue to grow. There will be more initiatives. There will be more champions. Success stories will bloom and spread. The best way to sum it all up is: where there is a collective will, there is always a way. That's what's next for women in baseball.

X. Conclusion

Reflection on the Journey

━━━━━━━

eveling the Playing Field has delved into the transformative expedition and gone on an inspiring journey of women breaking through the traditionally male-dominated world of Major League Baseball coaching and front office leadership. Many trailblazing women were interviewed. They all shared stories, challenges, their successes, advice and thoughts on female coaching and front office leadership.

There were lots of common themes in those interviews. The message of fighting for what someone wants came out loud and clear, regardless of gender.

Another thing that came out of this book is that baseball has recently progressed at a faster pace than before in regard to female inclusion in coaching and leadership. Some of those interviewed expressed their thoughts on getting to a point in time where female coaching is not a special topic of discussion. Some even said that they want to reach the point where they lose count of how many women coaches there are because there are so many, or at least many more. We are not there yet but are getting closer.

That made me think that maybe I'm too late in writing this book as female coaching is approaching being commonplace and no longer a special topic. I mentioned that to those interviewed and they all said passionately and strongly, "Please write the book. We are not there yet." They asked that I write their stories because there are still things yet to be done. MLB is trying but again, more is needed.

I refer back to what the Women's Sports Foundation said to the *Associated Press* about 2020 and female inclusion and trailblazing: "2020 was certainly a tumultuous and challenging year. It was also transformational, with many exciting, history-making firsts for women's sports, athletes, coaches, and leaders. Sports is a connector, a unifier, and a microcosm of society. As we reflect on the power of women athletes and teams who spoke up, challenged the norms, shattered glass ceilings, and showed girls, boys, and everyone the limitless potential one can achieve, it gives us all hope for the future." That hope continues to this day and the key words of achieving the limitless potential one can achieve is still paramount, in all of baseball.

For a long time, pioneering women in sports have worked to further progress and inspire others to accomplish history-defining athletic feats of their own. Include women coaching and working in the front office in Major League Baseball in that.

The early years tell a story of baseball heroes—pioneers who couldn't be brushed back, who dug in and played the game. Baseball transformed their lives. True, this is more about playing the game than coaching or being in the front office, but it still holds true. Just look at the transformed lives before us.

This book is written in the spirit of positivity, opportunity, and breakthroughs, not about all the reasons why something can't be done, gender interference, lack of inclusion and all the pushback related to not having women in baseball coaching. A lot is summed up in a recent social media hashtag by a post by the Cleveland Guardians: #inspireinclusion.

The story of women in sports is not a recent development but a complex history shaped by decades of persistence, determination, skill, and achievement. Despite enduring challenges such as gender stereotypes, discrimination, and financial disparities, women have played an integral role in the sports world, constantly pushing the limits of athletic accomplishment. This redefinition is evident today, particularly when we listen to individuals recounting their journeys, opportunities, challenges, and triumphs.

The push to bring women's sports to the masses started with names like Wilma Rudolph and Billie Jean King and has grown to include women like Lindsey Vonn, Danica Patrick, and Katie Ledecky. Now add to that list Kayla

Baptista, Veronica Alvarez, Alyssa Nakken, Katie Krall, and the many others whose stories are covered in *Leveling the Playing Field*.

Sport and baseball coaching, originally the exclusive domain of men, have changed throughout recent history thanks to milestones reached by women. Of course, some were victims of discrimination, but their fight and their achievements have set a precedent and they now are an inspiration for many others. Interest in women's sports has increased in, yet true equality remains a goal that requires further progress.

Every female coach we talked to emphasized that their efforts and their job are not about checking a gender box for their team. All would say that mindset didn't even come into play when interviewing or now while working. It's nice to hear that skills and aptitude were and are evaluated first and foremost. That's the spirit to continue with women in Major League Baseball.

Baseball, a beloved sport, thrives on inclusion, which shapes its core profoundly. Without this vital element, the cherished landscape of baseball would be different. The inclusion of individuals from diverse backgrounds and ethnicities has been the catalyst for its enduring impact, on the field and behind the scenes. Embracing diversity has allowed us to tap into a wide range of talents and perspectives, creating a dynamic and resilient baseball community. The spirit of inclusion strengthens the very fabric of our sport, ensuring that baseball remains a joyful and unified national pastime for all. With every pitch, swing of the bat, and fan's cheer, we celebrate an inclusive spirit that defines the heart and soul of baseball.

I leave you with this quote by another Arizonian, the late Sandra Day O'Connor, who served as an associate justice of the Supreme Court of the United States: "As society sees what women can do, as women see what women can do, there will be more women out there doing things, and we'll all be better off for it."

It is my hope that your interest in baseball and your interest in female inclusion in Major League Baseball and feelings about baseball mean much more now. It means more to me. I hope you had as much enjoyment reading this as I did in writing it. Thank you for reading *Leveling the Playing Field*.

About the Author: Al Lautenslager

A l has the ability to tell the stories necessary to connect with his audiences. From his personal experiences, he turns facts and chronology into innovative narratives. It is this quality that comes out in the writing of *Leveling the Playing Field*.

He is not only a well-known business author and contributor but has been an avid baseball fan since his youth, as either a spectator or a player. Growing up in Cincinnati before, during, and after the days of the Big Red Machine, Al put together a string of attending ten straight Cincinnati Reds opening day games. Opening Day in Cincinnati is a holiday. Al treated it as such and still marks the day on his calendar.

He has visited over half of the thirty Major League Baseball ballparks during his travels, in addition to visits to more than a dozen minor league games and parks. In 1983, Al drove to Philadelphia, attended Game 4 of the World Series against the Baltimore Orioles, and returned to his home in Dayton, Ohio, all in 24 hours' time, just because he was passionate about seeing the World Series that year. He has been to All-Star games and attended the very first game in the new Comiskey Park in Chicago.

In 1993, on a return plane trip from St. Louis to Chicago, Al had the privilege of sitting next to and enjoying a one-on-one conversation with hall-of-famer Lou Brock. Lou and Al talked about Pete Rose, the trade that brought Lou from Chicago to St. Louis, the Hall of Fame ring on his finger, and even life outside of baseball. This plane ride was a dream come true for any baseball fan. Al was able to live that dream.

Al met Pete Rose on the day he broke Ty Cobb's record with 4,192 hits. He was at the game in which Pete hit number 4,256, his last major league hit. In his home library, under a framed picture of the old Crosley Field in Cincinnati, his current baseball book collection contains every book ever written about Pete Rose, as well as volumes by Roger Angell, Roger Kahn, Bill James, Jonathan Eig, George Will, and many, many other baseball writers.

As an accomplished businessman, speaker, communicator, and author of travel and marketing books, Al understands the value of good publicity and promotion. As a result, he has built close ties to sports media, team representatives, and opinion makers.

Other Books by Al Lautenslager

- *Guerrilla Marketing in 30 Days*—Entrepreneur Media (best-seller and No. 1 on Amazon in Japan)
- *Guerrilla Marketing in 30 Days Workbook*—Entrepreneur Media
- *The Ultimate Guide to Direct Marketing*—Entrepreneur Media
- *Kick It Up A Notch Marketing*—Cameo Publications
- *RE: The Book*—Morgan James Publishing
- *Market Like You Mean It*—Entrepreneur Media
- *DaVinci Visits Today*—Self Published/Amazon
- *A Day in The Life Of A Tuscany Winemaker*—Self-Published/Amazon (Attained the No. 1 ranking on Amazon/Travel upon release)
- *Baseball Confidential*—Austin Macauley Publishing
- *Managing the Show*—Woodbridge Publishing

A free ebook edition is available with the purchase of this book.

To claim your free ebook edition:

1. Visit MorganJamesBOGO.com
2. Sign your name CLEARLY in the space
3. Complete the form and submit a photo of the entire copyright page
4. You or your friend can download the ebook to your preferred device

Print & Digital Together Forever.

Snap a photo

Free ebook

Read anywhere